© ASSOULINE, 1997
First published in France by Editions Assouline, 1996

First published in the the United States in 1997 by
UNIVERSE PUBLISHING
A Division of Rizzoli International Publications, Inc.
300 Park Avenue South, New York, NY 10010

English edition revised and updated.

Library of Congress Catalog Card Number: 97-61191

Design: Martin Fonquernie
Translated from the French by Molly Stevens
Copy-editing: Chanterelle Translations, London
Photo-engraving by Gravor, Switzerland
Printed and bound in Hong Kong

BASKET BALL

Eric Besnard
THE BEST OF NBA PHOTOGRAPHY

UNIVERSE

CONTENTS

success: in twelve years, merchandise sales shot up from 200 million dollars to 3.5 billion dollars. More important, the great money-making machine is now a great dream-creation machine, a phenomenon that has penetrated every sector of society. Basketball is not only a sport but a way of life, shared by millions of teenagers worldwide. The key to basketball's explosion is its players. Role models, with names like Larry Bird, Magic Johnson, and Michael Jordan, were promoted by David Stern even before they reached the height of their careers. In the 1980s, the Bird-Johnson duel captivated the United States, while Michael Jordan, who seems to redefine the laws of gravity, captured the world's attention soon after. Finally, as NBA Marketing Director Rick Welts notes, the creation of the Dream Team in 1992 has done more for the game than anything else in its one-hundred-year history.

Posters of the handful of players who appeared in Barcelona and Atlanta adorn the bedrooms of teenagers everywhere. They are the best basketball players of all time, champions of the world, and it is their stories that will be told in these pages, stories of the twists and turns in the lives of these players—stories that go beyond the magazine covers or the NBA stat sheets. Each of their astounding journeys is unique, as these are the players who have, in their own way, left their mark on the game and on the world. "There are some young players who are paid too much and don't respect the sport," said Jordan when he returned to the league. "I'm coming back to restore the real joy of playing, like Larry Bird, Magic Johnson, and a lot of others. The young need role models." These world champions come alive in this book.

HIST**ORY**

Springfield, Massachusetts. In 1891 the principal of the International YMCA Training School was looking for a good way to keep his students busy during the long winter days. He asked James Naismith, the physical education teacher, to think up some new ideas. It was not an easy task. However, a few months later, after a couple of failed experiments, Naismith had a brainstorm. Why not form two teams, take a ball that bounces, and set up two "goals" at a certain height at each end of the gym? The aim was to mix dexterity and strength. Naismith wrote out thirteen rules and posted them on the gym wall. The students loved the idea, and the next day they took two peach baskets and attached them to the gymnasium balcony on either side of the room. The teacher divided his class in two, assigning nine players to each side of the court, and the

THE STUFF HEROES ARE MADE OF
Mikan, Cousy and Havlicek playing for the Lakers and Celtics, the two most celebrated teams after World War II.

9

the game began. William Chase scored the only "goal" of the game—an historic basket—and his team won 1–0. Basketball was born.

But this was only the beginning. The YMCA spread the game throughout the United States. In 1896, a high school season was started in Colorado, and a professional league was formed in New Jersey, in which each player earned fifteen dollars per game—but the venture failed. Five years later, the first college league was created, and soon afterward, in 1909, the first international game in history was organized between the Russian Mayak Sports Club and the YMCA in Saint Petersburg. Later, during World War I, American G.I.'s brought basketball to Europe, increasing its popularity there. In 1932, the International Basketball Federation was founded.

Sharp cultural differences, however, brought international expansion to a sudden end. It was soon apparent that the United States was in a league of its own, and that basketball was firmly rooted in American culture. For many Americans, the game represented the promise of a better life for successful players—but for the rest of the world it was just a game. By the end of World War II, the world's basketball stars were American and they came out of what would come to be known as the NBA.

The NBA story begins on June 6, 1946, with the founding of the Basketball Association of America at the Commodore Hotel in New York. Maurice Podoloff was president. Hoping to inject more action into the game, the league, which included the New York Knicks and the Boston Celtics, prohibited zone defense. Seventeen teams joined the association at the beginning of the 1946 season. Soon afterwards, however, six teams withdrew because of financial problems. Philadelphia won the first championship, but money continued to plague the BAA. Luckily, the National Basketball League, a weak rival that was also financially challenged, declared bankruptcy in 1949. On August 3, the BAA picked up the six remaining teams from the NBL and adopted the name the National Basketball Association.

The first big player in the NBA was the 6'10" George Mikan, star of the 1950s, who made seven thousand dollars per year. In his nine years with the Minneapolis Lakers, number 99 led his team to five championship titles and played in the All-NBA First Team six consecutive times. "We couldn't stop him," remembered his opponents. There was no one like Mikan. Legend has it that one day when the Lakers were playing at Madison Square Garden against the New York Knicks, the team came upon a sign at the door to the court that read, "Tonight, Mikan vs. the Knicks."

Little by little, the NBA rules were refined. The draft appeared, allowing poorly ranked teams to have first pick of new players, and in 1954, Danny Biasone, owner of Syracuse's team, came up with the the twenty-four-second rule. Biasone wanted a quicker game and a better show. Why twenty-four seconds? "By figuring the average number of shots two teams would take during the game, which was about 120, and dividing that into the length of the game, which was about forty-eight minutes, or 2,880 seconds, you come up with twenty-four." In addition to these refinements, an extra free throw was granted after five team fouls in every quarter.

By the end of the 1950s, the Boston Celtics replaced the Minneapolis Lakers at

JAMES NAISMITH, THE INVENTOR

The gym teacher thinks up the game of basketball in 1891 in hopes of keeping his students occupied during the long days of winter.

the top and would go on to dominate the rest of the league. In ten years, they won the title nine times, eight of which were consecutive. Their coach, Red Auerbach, was a wizard. In 1956, he dared to trade away star players Ed Macauley and Cliff Hagan to St. Louis for draft pick Bill Russell. (Auerbach would later call Russell the best player in basketball's history.) When he joined Boston, the 6'9" Bill Russell had just won two college titles with San Francisco, as well as the gold medal with the United States Olympic team in Melbourne. It did not take long to prove that Auerbach was right to draft him. In his first game on December 22, 1956, Russell grabbed sixteen rebounds in twenty-one minutes and blocked three of Bob Petit's shots in the last quarter. Russell, unlike Mikan, did not rely on his height alone. He was agile and a born leader. "He made us better," said Tom Sanders, his old teammate. Russell finished first in rebounds for four seasons and took Boston to nine championship titles before becoming the first African-American coach in NBA history, taking Red Auerbach's place. In 1968 and 1969, he landed the championship as both coach and player.

At Russell's side was Bob Cousy, "Houdini of the Hardwood," a magician and a

THE FIRST SANCTUM

The YMCA International Training School where the game was invented.

INTRODUCTION

Perhaps the single most telling indicator of the actual extent of the global basketball craze is the fact that 71 percent of the world's teenagers watch or play the game, while only 64 percent are interested in soccer (as reported by a June 1996 survey conducted by the Brainwaves Group, a branch of DMB&B Communications Worldwide, among 25,057 teenagers between the ages of fifteen and eighteen in forty-one countries). Whereas only fifteen years ago NBA finals were pre-recorded and shown abroad only in Europe, today the games are televised live in 169 countries to more than 600 million viewers, of whom close to 60 million are Americans! After the Olympics, the World Cup, and the Super Bowl, basketball is the most highly-publicized and televised sporting event in the world.

The NBA owes its success to many individuals, especially to Commissioner David Stern. When Stern took over the league in 1984, it was he who came up with the visionary idea of tapping the global market through televised matches. Merchandising was the obvious next step. NBA products were a runaway

player of dazzling achievement. He led the Celtics to six championships, was leader in assists eight times, and finished his career with an average of 18.4 points per game. He also played in thirteen straight All-Star Games. After losing the championship to Philadelphia in 1967, the Celtics won the following two seasons, but their dynasty fell in 1969. Such a team would never be seen again.

In the 1960s, the NBA was expanding quickly. Other leagues were surfacing, like the American Basketball League (ABL), which introduced the three-point shot in 1961. But two years later, it filed for bankruptcy. The American Basketball Association (ABA), which played with a red-white-and-blue ball, eventually faced the same misfortune. It would also try to promote the three-point shot (not instituted until 1979 in the NBA) and was somewhat successful thanks to its commissioner, George Mikan. Even though the ABA snatched players, coaches, and referees from the NBA, the league collapsed in 1975.

In the 1960s, the NBA legend flourished with players like Oscar Robertson, the "Big O." Robertson is the only player in history to have completed a season with a triple-double average: 30.8 points, 12.5 rebounds, and 11.4 assists in 1962. Two years later, he fell only seven rebounds short of repeating this feat. But Robertson has said that records did not interest him. If Jordan hadn't come along, Robertson might well have been the best all-around player in basketball history. Unfortunately, the Milwaukee Bucks weren't able to back up Robertson's talent until 1971, when Kareem Abdul-Jabbar joined their ranks. Robertson only landed one championship, but was a six-time leader in assists and was Most Valuable Player in 1964.

Robertson's exceptional all-around performance can never be equaled, but the feats of one of his contemporaries are just as impressive: In 1962, Wilt Chamberlain averaged a tremendous fifty-plus points per game. He had also succeeded in reaching 65 points twice and 67 points twice. His extraordinary performances were commonplace, but on March 4, 1962 he exceeded his best efforts. Facing the New York Knicks, Chamberlain scored 23 points twelve minutes into the game. At half time, he scored 41. Philadelphia Warrior coach Frank McGuire, sat on the edge of his seat in the second period, watching Chamberlain continue to stack up the points. During a time-out, he announced

THE FIRST HEROES

*Bill Russell (far left): in 1980, the Celtics'
number 6 is named "best player in history."
"Dr. J"(left): He seemed to remain in a state
of levitation. Kareem Abdul-Jabbar (below):
with his famous sky hook, it was impossible to
stop him. Wilt Chamberlain (bottom):
the only player to score
a 100-point game.*

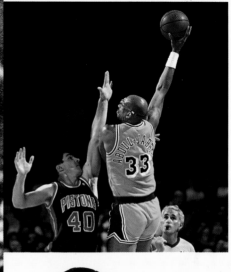

15

that all shots should go to Chamberlain. With twelve minutes left in the game, Chamberlain had 69 points. The four thousand fans in the stadium were on their feet. With forty-five seconds to go, Chamberlain dunked his 100th point.

At 7'1" Chamberlain was able to jump higher and run faster than anyone in the league. His ability earned him an unprecedented one hundred thousand dollars plus per year. He averaged 37.6 points and 27 rebounds his first season, led in scoring for seven consecutive years, was first in rebounds eleven times, and earned MVP honors four times. Chamberlain had joined the Harlem Globetrotters before even completing school, and he went on to play in two championships, in 1967 and 1972, with two of the best teams of the century, the Philadelphia Warriors and the Los Angeles Lakers. There was only one man that could stop Chamberlain—Bill Russell. According to Bob Petit, no one had ever scored like Chamberlain and no one had ever defended like Russell. They were stars not only for their generation, but for all time. Chamberlain's teams, however, didn't dominate the era as did Bill Russell's Celtics. Many other teams, including the New York Knicks, were able to snatch the championship in the early 1970s, which was also a time when new franchises emerged. It was a turning point, not least of all because it was the moment Julius Erving and Kareem Abdul-Jabbar appeared.

Born Lew Alcindor, Kareem Abdul-Jabbar dominated basketball for 20 years. He began by capturing three consecutive NCAA championship titles with UCLA, finishing his three-year college career with an 88–2 record. Before participating in the NBA draft in 1969, he converted to Islam and changed his name. In 1969, the Milwaukee Bucks won the first draft pick and signed Abdul-Jabbar for seven years. In his first game, he scored 29 points, grabbed 12 rebounds, and had 6 important assists. In 1971, he led Milwaukee to their first title ever. But in 1975, he left the Bucks, joining the Los Angeles Lakers. Abdul-Jabbar's favorite weapon was the sky hook, an arched arm shot that Pat Riley, ex-Lakers' coach, and Larry Bird have called the best offensive weapon in modern basketball. Before leaving basketball on June 14, 1989, at the age of 42, Abdul-Jabbar had a career total of more than 44,000 points and 20,000 rebounds. In addition, he had earned six NBA titles, six league MVP Awards, and two Finals

MVP Awards in 1975 and 1985. Only one contemporary player left as big an impression on American fans—Julius Erving, "Dr. J."

Erving was the first player to appear to hang in mid-air. "He seemed to be levitating," recalls player Billy Paultz, "and I know that's not possible, but I swear that's what he did." He was the Jordan of his time, finding possibilities everywhere. "Dr. J" was one of the seven players in history to average more than twenty points and twenty rebounds in college. Oddly enough, he began his professional career in the ABA (the NBA rival) with the Virginia Squires, before joining the New York Nets and leading them to the championships with 28.7 points and 12.1 rebounds per game. When the ABA collapsed, he joined the NBA's Philadelphia 76ers. In 1983, Erving was the only player who could stop Magic Johnson and Larry Bird. Bird said he hated to lose, but if it was against Philadelphia, it was alright, because of Julius Erving.

THE SPRINGFIELD GYM (below)
William Chase gets the first basket in history in December 1891.
THE OTHER DREAM TEAM (following pages)
The very first team. James Naismith is to the right in
the second row and William Chase is the fourth player
from the left in the third row.

Erving and Jabbar marked the end of an era, and Magic and Bird introduced another—one full of risk and flair, one in which records were set. Jordan dominates the game, and Charles Barkley destroys backboards. The NBA discovered Shaquille O'Neal, and the Dream Team was formed. Basketball is now known in every part of the world. William Chase is a player lost in the history books. For the nineties have marked a new beginning.

"Air Jordan"

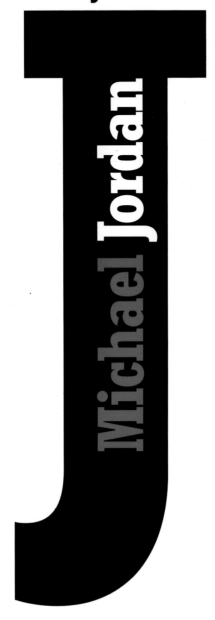

It was Sunday, June 16, 1996. Father's Day. The Chicago–Seattle finals had just ended. Michael Jordan grabbed hold of the game ball and ran towards the United Center's locker room, the press at his back. He was alone. It was a beautiful moment. The greatest player of all time lay face down on the floor and cried. After his first championship victory in 1991, his father had held him in his arms for a long time. Five years later, Jordan savored his fourth trophy. His achievements were unprecedented. At this moment, he no longer focused on the cameras or the handful of photographers at his heels. He squeezed the ball even harder, kissed and stroked it. He reviewed the past few years: his farewell to basketball, his flirtation with baseball, his amazing comeback, and especially the death of his father, which was the greatest tragedy of his life. "I thought about him more today than ever," he said. "It was probably the worst day to have the game. My heart and soul were elsewhere, but the team was great. They helped me along. I would have liked for him to see this."

The great story of Michael Jeffrey Jordan started on February 17, 1963, in Brooklyn. His father, James, worked in a nuclear power plant in Wilmington, North Carolina. He came to New York for a training session, accompanied by his pregnant wife, Deloris. Upon learning of the death of her mother, Deloris gave birth prematurely. Michael Jordan was already ahead of his time.

MICHAEL JORDAN/AIR JORDAN
Born February 17, 1963, in Brooklyn, New York/6'6" 216 lbs/High School: Laney High School, Wilmington, North Carolina/College: North Carolina/NCAA Championship in 1982/Selected by the Chicago Bulls in the first round (third overall pick)/NBA Rookie of the Year in 1985/NBA championship with the Chicago Bulls in 1991, 1992, 1993, 1996 and 1997/Leader in points scored in 1987, 1988, 1989, 1990, 1991, 1992, 1993, 1996 and 1997/Defensive Player of the Year in 1988/Leader in steals in 1988, 1990 and 1993/League MVP in 1988, 1991, 1992 and 1996/NBA Finals MVP in 1991, 1992, 1993, 1996 and 1997/All-NBA First Team in 1987, 1988, 1989, 1990, 1991, 1992, 1993, 1996 and 1997/All-Defensive First Team in 1988, 1989, 1990, 1991, 1992, 1993, 1996 and 1997/Eleven All-Star Game appearances and MVP in 1988 and 1996/Won the slam dunk contest in 1987 and 1988/Gold medal in the 1984 Olympic Games/Member of Dream Team I

The family and the work ethic were sacred to the Jordans. James Jordan was a foreman at General Electric, and Deloris Jordan worked as the head of customer relations at a bank. The kids worked for pocket money in the summer, but Michael couldn't stand it. He hated the routine.

He was a good student and a promising athlete at Virgo High School. In his first year, he divided his time between football, baseball, and basketball, excelling at all three sports. When he transferred to Laney High his sophomore year, he was too short to make the basketball team. At 5'10", Michael Jordan had to play on the reserve team in order to get game time. His coach Fred Lynch still laughs about it today, "We'll never have another reserve team like it." Michael didn't aspire to join the NBA, because baseball was really his first love. Maybe his father would get to see him play professional ball.

Everything started to change in his last two years of high school. Michael, who had grown to 6'4", lay down his bat and became the star of the high school basketball team. Laney won the conference for the first time, and Jordan played in the High School All-Star Game with the top high school players in the country. History was in the making.

James Jordan followed his son everywhere, advising and training him. At eighteen, Michael decided to join Dean Smith at the University of North Carolina. Smith reviewed the basics, and Jordan worked hard. He was arrogant, but his talents came through immediately. The coach of North Carolina State, Jim Valvano, said that if God had given one athlete all the talents on earth, that athlete was Michael Jordan. During Jordan's freshman year, he and the Tar Heels took the 1982 championship. Jordan scored the game-winning basket in the final seconds against Patrick Ewing and the Georgetown Hoyas—a 63–62 victory. Jordan said it was this basket that gave him confidence for his upcoming career. He applied himself the following two years, jumping from 13.5 points per game to 20, and was named twice in the NCAA's annual top five. In addition, he was chosen by Bobby Knight to play in the Los Angeles Olympic Games, where he won his first gold medal, scoring an average of 17.1 points. Jordan was young, but felt confident that he could meet the challenges of the NBA.

Jordan's draft was marked by an enormous blunder. Believing a strong team depended on the center, Houston chose Hakeem Olajuwon as their first pick. But Portland made the mistake of the century by selecting the tall Sam Bowie over Michael Jordan. In the fall of 1984, Jordan packed his bags for the Windy City. His first five-year contract was worth four million dollars, an unprecedented amount for a guard, but the Bulls were a failing team, and were counting on Jordan to get them back on their feet. They wouldn't be disappointed. In his third game, Jordan totaled 37 points against Milwaukee. In only one month, he became the team's leader in points, rebounds, and steals. The crumbling Chicago stadium turned around financially, and Jordan was chosen to start in the NBA All-Star Game in Indianapolis. But Jordan was not prepared for what he would encounter at the game. Larry Bird, Magic Johnson, and Isiah Thomas had decided to teach the newcomer a lesson. They kept the ball away

IN THE NAME OF THE FATHER (below)
The Jordan clan. Michael, his mother Doloris and his father and role model, James.
A NUMBER FOR THE HISTORY BOOKS (p. 31)
After Jordan's leave in 1993, Chicago retires his uniform. When he returns in 1995
he takes number 45 for a couple of games to start fresh. The last number
that Jordan's father saw him play with was number 23.

In August,
his father,
James, was found
murdered.
Jordan's world
collapsed.
He realized
how quickly
people can
disappear
and decided
it was time
to get back
to a more
normal life.

CHICAGO BULLS

23

MICHAEL JORDAN
1984-1993

JORDAN

45

from Jordan, and the brash young man scored only seven points. Jordan was bitter about this for a long time. Despite the episode, he brought the Bulls to their first playoffs in forty years, and was named NBA Rookie of the Year with an average of 28.2 points (third best in the NBA) and 6.5 rebounds in 82 games. What followed was a series of uninterrupted titles and records. In 1986, despite a foot injury that eliminated him for part of the season, Jordan came back to rack up 63 points against the Celtics, an NBA playoff record. In the locker room, Larry Bird said, "It's God disguised as Jordan." Things only improved from there. Sell-out crowds came to see the Bulls, and, in 1987, Jordan was the first player to receive more than one million votes for the All-Star Game. On that day, he flew through the air to win his first NBA Slam Dunk Championship. He scored 40 points during the game.

THE END OF THE WORLD (below)

October 6, 1993. Press conference at Deerfield, Illinois. Jordan stands with his wife Juanita and announces that the time has come for him to step away from the game.

ALONE IN THE WORLD (pp. 36–37)

End of the 1996 Finals against Seattle. Father's Day. After the game, Jordan takes the ball, throws himself on the floor, and cries.

Jordan's popularity grew beyond sports, as major companies fought for his sponsorship. Nike, the first to sign Jordan, gave him a nine-year contract for twenty million dollars. Wilson, Gatorade, Wheaties, Hanes, McDonald's, Chevrolet, and Upper Deck signed him on as well. His non-basketball income exceeded thirty-five million dollars per year.

In the seasons to follow, Jordan monopolized money, glory, and records. He was Defensive Player of the Year and NBA leader in points scored. But one thing was missing—the NBA championship title that would establish his legitimacy. Jerry Krause flanked Jordan with Scottie Pippen and Horace Grant in 1987, but it wasn't until Phil Jackson replaced Doug Collins as coach in 1990 that the Jordan revolution began. Jackson asked Jordan to shoot a little less in order to build teamwork and plays, including the old triangle attack system that gave each player more opportunity to shoot. Jordan agreed to the plan, and the team matured. Pippen and Grant became All-Stars, as the Bulls won one game after another. The Bulls achieved a "three-peat" between 1991 and 1993, winning the NBA Championship against the Lakers, the Blazers, and the Suns. Chicago was *the* team of the 1990s, and both Jordan and Pippen harvested Olympic gold in Barcelona. But despite Jordan's success, "His Airness" was subjected to incessant attacks regarding his gambling debts. The summer of 1993 would be hell for Jordan.

In August 1993, Jordan's father, James, was found murdered on the side of a highway, and the star's world collapsed. On October 6, Jordan called a press conference at Deerfield, Chicago's training center. Most of his teammates stood dumbfounded as Jordan announced he was leaving basketball. He wanted time to step back from the game. Though he admitted he loved basketball, and always would, he felt that he had reached his goal at this particular time in his life. He didn't have anything else to prove. The death of his father made him realize how quickly people can disappear from one's life. It was time for him to be more generous, spend more time with his family, wife and children, and to recapture a more normal life.

A few weeks later, however, Michael Jordan announced his return to sports. This time he was heading for a baseball field—a childhood dream, one shared by his father. Jordan said that everything he accomplished was dedicated to his father, who always thought he could be a Major Leaguer. He always told Jordan, "You never know until you try," and that's exactly what his son did. After signing with the Chicago White Sox, he was assigned to the farm team, the Birmingham Barons. Jordan's baseball career became a lesson in humility. Jordan learned to be patient and to accept the limits of certain players more easily, no matter what the game. During spring training with the Scottsdale Scorpions he made no apparent progress. On March 2, 1995, after an unremarkable White Sox pre-season outing, Jordan gave up baseball. Soon after, rumor spread of his return to the NBA.

In 1995, Jordan began training again with the Bulls. He returned to play after a brief announcement: "I'm back." The very next day Jordan scored 19 points against the Pacers, and a few days later another 55 against the Knicks at Madison Square Garden. Only a few cynics thought he returned a weaker player. The only thing that really changed for Jordan was his number. He returned wearing "45." His father had last seen him play in "23"—but that chapter had ended. However, in view of his bumpy start, a staff member suggested that Jordan take back number "23." Jordan accepted. That year the Bulls were eliminated in the playoffs by the Orlando Magic, but Jordan, who averaged 26.9 points in seventeen games, knew he still had it. He averaged 32.3 points over ten years. Jordan downplayed his accomplishments.

On the night of June 16, 1996, Michael Jordan led the NBA in points for the eighth time, and was both League MVP and Finals MVP for a fourth time. Chicago won its fourth title. During the game against Seattle, Jordan's children, Jeffrey, Marcus, and Jasmine, waved a sign that read, "Happy Birthday Dad!" Jordan savored the moment. He wore a World Champions cap and puffed on a cigar while answering reporters who pounded him with questions. The trophy was at his side, glistening. "Who's it for?" asked a journalist. Michael Jordan stared at the prized object. "My family, my kids, and their grandfather." Jordan basked in the moment. Suddenly, he raised his eyes to the sky, as if remembering that he was not alone. He paused, smiled, and added, "You know, I'm happy to be back."

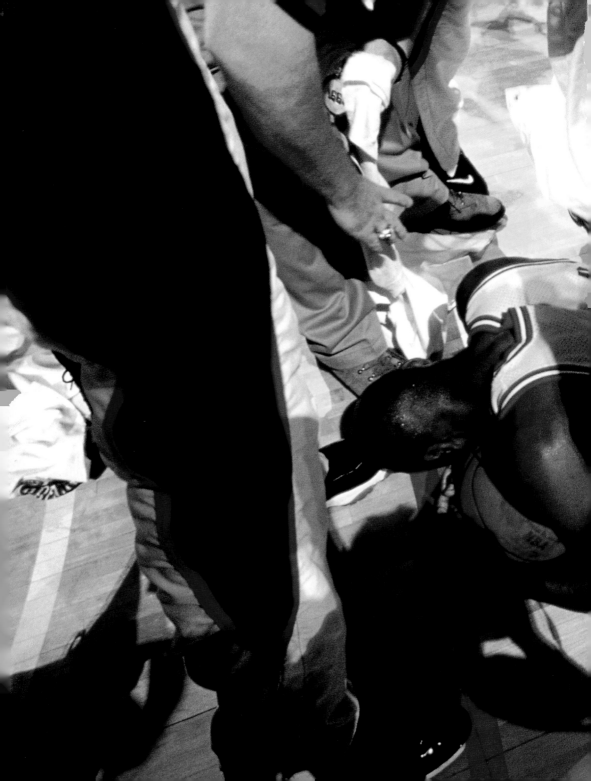

One year and thirty million dollars later, Jordan led the Bulls to a fifth title against Utah. He was the best player in the finals, the highest points scorer, and the best defensive player, yet all these achievements seemed almost anecdotal. " I felt forced to lead this team to its fifth title" Jordan asserted. "I'll never play for any coach but Jackson, and I want Scottie to get what he deserves," added the greatest player of all time. "One more year!" chanted the spectators in the United Center. The myth lives on.

MICHAEL JORDAN

CHICAGO BULLS
1984 — 1993

The best there ever was. The best there ever will be.

"Magic"

Earvin Johnson

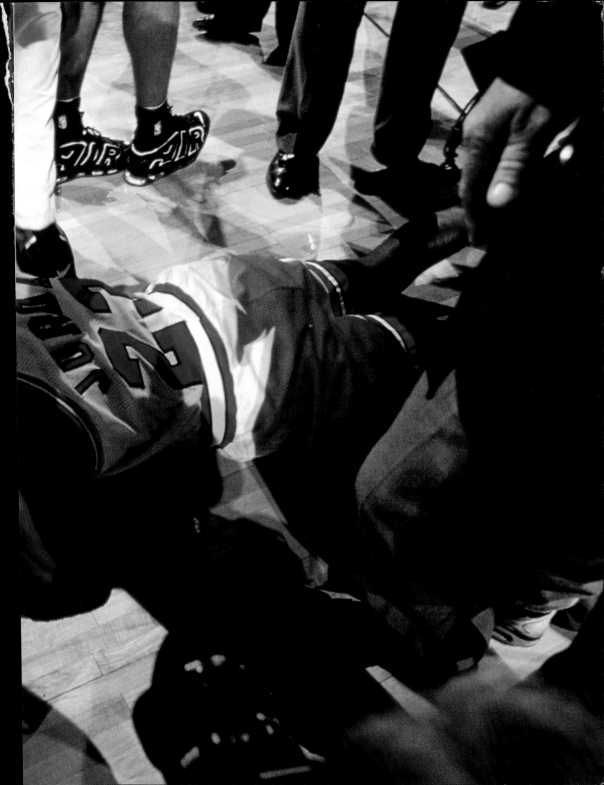

November 7, 1991, is an unforgettable day in the history of basketball. The Los Angeles Lakers called a press conference at the Great Western Forum in Inglewood. Magic Johnson was there, flanked by his wife Cookie, NBA Commissioner David Stern, and Kareem Abdul-Jabbar, the other Lakers' icon and one of Magic's best friends. A little before four o'clock, Magic announced, "I have contracted the HIV virus…I have to leave the Lakers immediately. I want to emphasize that I don't have full-blown AIDS, but I am HIV positive." Silence followed. "I'm going to become a spokesperson for people with the virus," he added. "I'm here to tell you that it can happen to anybody, even me. I will definitely miss basketball, but you'll see me hanging around the court. See you soon." Radio and television stations interrupted their regular programs to announce the news. The country was in a state of shock. That very night at Madison Square Garden, the crowd recited the Lord's Prayer in unison, and Pat Riley, Magic's old coach, reminded fans that Magic was still alive and needed everyone's love more than ever. During the national anthem in Chicago, the giant screen that hangs over the floor read, "Magic, we love you." Magic was in the hearts of all Americans. He was the pride of the country, a role model. Many suddenly realized that AIDS was more than just another unfortunate statistic in the newspaper. It had a face, and a name. Magic was a friend whose smile and freshness had brought joy to basketball. He was a magician. He

EARVIN JOHNSON/MAGIC
Born on August 14, 1959 in Lansing, Michigan/6'9" 255 lbs/High School: Everett High School, Lansing/College: Michigan State/NCAA Champion in 1979/Most Outstanding Player of the NCAA Finals in 1979/Drafted by the Los Angeles Lakers in 1979 (first overall pick)/Wins NBA championship title with the Lakers in 1980, 1982, 1985, 1987 and 1988/Leader in steals in 1981 and 1982/Leader in assists in 1983, 1984, 1986 and 1987/Best free thrower in 1989/MVP in 1987, 1989 and 1990/NBA Finals MVP in 1980, 1982 and 1987/All-NBA First Team in 1983, 1984, 1985, 1986, 1987, 1988, 1989, 1990 and 1991/Twelve All-Star Game appearances; MVP in 1990 and 1992/Member of Dream Team I

was the only player Larry Bird would pay to see play.

Magic's story started in Lansing, Michigan, where he was born Earvin Johnson on August 14, 1959. His family called him Junior. Lansing is a working-class town outside of Detroit. Earvin Senior had two jobs to support his wife and ten children. Earvin Jr. also did his share of odd jobs. At ten years old, he raked up leaves, mowed lawns, and trimmed hedges in the neighborhood; at fifteen, he was the weekend night guard for two big companies in the area, Ferguson and Easton. "I remember," he said, "as soon as the place cleared out, I'd pretend to be the owner. I'd sit in the boss's chair, put my feet up on the desk, and pretend to give out orders to invisible workers." He dreamed of becoming a businessman. He would hold on to that wish.

He was a wizard with a basketball. At Everett High School, he played all positions well and began to carve out a solid reputation for himself. One day in 1974, Earvin nailed 36 points, grabbed 18 rebounds, made 16 assists, and had 20 steals against Jackson Parkside. No one had ever seen anything like it. Fred Stabley Jr., who covered basketball for the *Lansing State Journal*, rushed to the locker room after the game. "Earvin, we need to find you a nickname. What do you think of 'Magic'?" A legend was born.

In 1977, he attended Michigan State so he could be close to his hometown and family. In his two years there, he led the Spartans to win the Big Ten Conference for the first time since 1959 and also took them to the NCAA title in his second year! In the final game of that year, Johnson went head-to-head

MAGIC JOHNSON

47

with Larry Bird. Everyone picked their favorite, and the country would be divided for the next ten years. Michigan State beat Indiana State 75 to 64 in the final, and Magic, who scored 24 points (7 rebounds), was elected Most Valuable Player. Under Magic's wand, Michigan State had a state record of 51 and 11, and Johnson left college averaging a remarkable 17.1 points, 7.6 rebounds, and 7.9 assists per game, which placed him at the top of every category in the league. It was rare to see a guard with such statistics. At 6'9", Magic Johnson changed the position forever, partly by instituting new tricks like the blind pass. No one knew what he would do next. He had a sixth sense for each game. He could dribble across the most difficult terrain, and had a quarterback's arm, his ultimate weapon. Pat Riley called him the blank piece in Scrabble, the one that could substitute for any other piece.

On June 25, 1979, the Los Angeles Lakers took home the championship title. Three years earlier, they had let go of the aging Gail Goodrich to the New Orleans Jazz in exchange for three draft picks. The trade seemed insignificant, but the Jazz had a very poor 1978–79 season and the NBA gave them first overall pick in 1979. The Lakers made the most of the situation, and a dream came true. The three thousand seats in the Lakers' gym weren't enough to accommodate the crowd that gathered to witness Magic Johnson's first practice session. Magic was all smiles. However, teammates like Kareem Abdul-Jabbar couldn't bear to see the kid from Michigan take center stage and pocket twenty-five million dollars over twenty-five years. The grudge wouldn't last though.

In Magic's first season, the Lakers met Julius Erving and the Philadelphia 76ers in the finals. In the fifth game, unfortunately, Abdul-Jabbar, who had scored 40 points, twisted his ankle. It was a tough break. Los Angeles was winning three games to two, but they were worried about battling the 76ers without their 7'2" star. But their guard, Magic, the blank Scrabble piece, played center. After forty-eight minutes, the rookie scored 42 points, 15 rebounds, 7 assists, 5 steals, and 1 block. The Lakers won, and Magic became the first rookie to be named MVP. Suns' coach Cotton

Fitzsimmons claimed that Magic put the Lakers in a league of their own. The next year, Pat Riley, who replaced Paul Westhead as the Lakers' coach, picked James Worthy in the first round of the 1982 draft. From that point on, Magic cleaned up in the NBA: five championship titles, three Finals MVP awards, three MVP honors for the regular season, leader in assists four times, twice in steals, and once in free-throws. He was named nine times to the All-NBA First Team and played in the All-Star Game twelve times. Everything seemed to be going his way until that terrible day in November of 1991 when in his farewell address he said, "You'll see me hanging around the court." But he loved basketball too much to let it go completely.

To keep in shape, he lifted weights and played in a couple of games. In 1992, the country voted for him to play in the All-Star Game, where he stood out by racking up 25 points, 5 rebounds, and 9 assists. David Stern announced afterwards, "You're the best player in this game and the

SHOWTIME!
The face of the Lakers in the early eighties: Magic Johnson (with towel around neck) and Kareem Abdul-Jabbar (number 33).

bravest person I know. This moment is yours." Magic received a standing ovation. Four months later, he was asked to play on the Dream Team in Barcelona—a unique opportunity—Magic would become the hero of the Games. When he returned to the United States, he joined the Lakers' spring training, hoping to play in the 1992–93 season. However, several players announced their concern about playing with an HIV-infected player. At the end of March 1994, Johnson nevertheless acted as coach for the now weakened Lakers. The first game at the Forum against Milwaukee was sold out. Jack Nicholson took his usual seat in the first row, and Los Angeles won 110–101. But the "Magic touch" didn't last. After five wins in six outings, the team crumbled, not even making it to the playoffs for

LARGER THAN LIFE

Magic and Jordan, the most accomplished players of all time,
head-to-head at the time of Magic's return in February 1996.

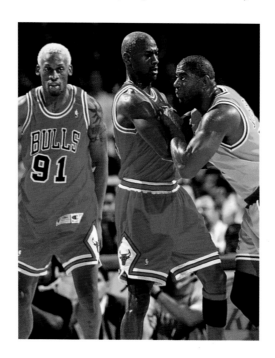

the first time since 1976. Magic felt lost, and complained that the young players no longer wanted to win. He knew he couldn't win with this team, even though he longed to. "History can't win us games. I'm leaving."

Magic was frustrated and turned to his old dream of becoming a businessman. He had earned over one hundred million dollars and was looking to become co-owner of a basketball franchise, like Sacramento, Toronto, or Los Angeles. Lakers' owner Jerry Buss sold him five percent of the team shares and made him vice-president. He also invested in cinema complexes (the Magic Johnson Theater) and flirted with sportswear manufacturing. All along, he continued to fight AIDS, criss-crossing the world, fundraising for the cause. Every now and then, he would play with a team of old stars, but even though he kept busy, Magic missed the real thing.

On January 26, 1996, Magic announced that he had signed with the Lakers for one more season. "It's now or never," he said. "I want my son to see me play." Two days later, he played against the Golden State Warriors at the Forum. The Lakers turned down fifty thousand requests for seats and could only allow three hundred journalists into the event that would be broadcast around the world. TNT registered the highest ratings for an NBA game, and tickets were scalped for more than two thousand dollars a piece. Magic confessed he was as nervous as he had been for his first game in 1979.

Although Johnson had put on more than twenty-five pounds, and he was a bit slower, he still managed to score 19 points, 10 assists, and 8 rebounds in 27 minutes. He was just two rebounds short of a triple-double. "If I were a little younger," he claimed, "I think I would do a back-flip right here, I'm so happy. God has heard my prayers." Most people were skeptical, however. Scottie Pippen, the Bulls' forward, warned that it was too early to get excited about Magic's return. How long would Magic last? Despite some good performances, Magic didn't have quite the same impact on the game as before. Lakers coach Dell Harris made him play forward because he knew that Magic wasn't fast enough to beat the guards of the day. Magic was on the bench at the start of the playoffs and was over-

November 7, 1991. Magic announces that he has contracted the HIV virus and declares he is leaving the Lakers the same day. His wife Cookie is at his side.

looked for Dream Team III in Atlanta. The magic was fading. In May 1996, he retired again.

Whatever happens next, Magic knows his most important battle is now the one against the fearsome AIDS virus. If he can't beat it, he will at least send the fight into over-time—for himself and for others. He doesn't want people to feel sorry for him. He has said, "Even if I die tomorrow, I'll have had a great life." His courage is an admirable lesson in dignity.

Hakeem Olajuwon
"The Dream"

It's no surprise that David Stern picked Hakeem Olajuwon to be the NBA's Ambassador to the World. A Muslim, originally from Nigeria, Olajuwon is proof that the NBA is universal—as is basketball. He is the first African to carve out a place in the American pros. He is also a man of wisdom with a big heart. His nickname is "The Dream," but he is a nightmare for his opponents. Olajuwon is one of the best two or three players in the game.

Olajuwon didn't start to play basketball until he was fifteen years old. Still living in Lagos, Nigeria, he was goalie for the soccer and handball teams at his high school, the Muslim Teacher's College. But since the basketball team didn't have any tall players, he was asked to join the team the night before an inter-school final game. This became a major turning point. Akeem (his name was then spelled without an "H") was to become one of the best players in the country.

Two years later, he was picked to be on the national team for the Pan-African Games. Guy Lewis (the coach at University of Houston) had a friend at the games who spotted Olajuwon and called Lewis immediately. The usual endless discussions and negotiations followed, but Akeem was ready to leave for Houston within the next couple of months.

Olajuwon knew he had a lot to learn and therefore spent his first year working hard in his classes (especially learning English) and practicing. His work was cut out for him since he knew it would take more than his 7'0" to make the starting five.

But it didn't take him long to show his stuff. He could do everything. He was great on defense, rebounding, and blocking shots, and had no problem playing

HAKEEM OLAJUWON/THE DREAM
Born on January 21, 1963 in Lagos, Nigeria/7'1" 250 lbs/High School: Muslim Teachers College, Lagos/College: University of Houston/NBA Championship winner with the Houston Rockets in 1994 and 1995/Leader in rebounds in 1989 and 1990/Leader in blocked shots in 1990, 1991 and 1993/Defensive Player of the Year in 1993 and 1994/League MVP in 1994/NBA Finals MVP in 1994 and 1995/All-NBA First Team in 1987, 1988, 1989, 1994 and 1997/Member of the All-Defensive First Team in 1987, 1988, 1990, 1993 and 1994/Twelve All-Star Game appearances/Member of Dream Team III

THE UNIQUE CLASS OF 1981 IS NICKNAMED PHI SLAMMA JAMMA. OLAJUWON PLAYS CENTER

center for the Cougars. But the team name wouldn't last. The exceptional class of 1981 would be renamed for college basketball history: Phi Slamma Jamma.

Phi Slamma Jamma was "The Philosophy of Slamming and Jamming," otherwise known as the fraternity of awesome dunkers. A *Houston Post* journalist thus anointed the team because of their fast game, highlighted by a lot of slamming: 194 dunks in 1984, 85 by Olajuwon. On the Houston roster was not only Akeem Olajuwon, but also Clyde Drexler, Michael Young (who would be European champion in 1993 with the team from Limoges, France), Larry Micheaux, Alvin Franklin, and Benny Anders. Only a year before, these players were hardly known, but in their four years they instilled fear in college teams across the country. They didn't win anything, however. In 1982, Olajuwon and Houston fell to Jordan and North Carolina in the semifinals of the Final Four. The following year, North Carolina State beat them in the finals, with a last-second basket by Lorenzo Charles. Despite his team's loss Olajuwon was nevertheless selected "MVP of the Final Four," an honor almost never awarded to someone on the losing team. In 1984, Houston lost again in the finals, this time to Patrick Ewing and Georgetown. But Olajuwon was unmatched in his position: in 1983–84, he led in rebounds (13.5 per game), and blocked shots (5.6), and had the highest field goal percentage (67.5 percent) in college basketball. "When Hakeem is on," explained Drexler, who left the Cougars in 1983, "all you have to do is pass him the ball and watch him go."

The Houston Rockets chose Olajuwon as their number one pick in the 1984 draft over Sam Bowie and Michael Jordan. Olajuwon and Ralph Sampson became the most effective inside duo in the NBA, notching up more than twenty points and ten rebounds each in their first season together. In 1986, the "Twin Towers" led Houston to the NBA finals against the legendary Boston Celtics. Olajuwon was outstanding (averaging 25.5 points), but it wasn't enough to give the Rockets the win. They lost four games to two, as Larry Bird and his team pocketed another title.

Hakeem (who added the "H" to his name in 1991) hadn't won any championships in six years and was becoming disheartened. In early 1992, he got angry and asked his managers to quadruple his salary (which was already more than three million dollars). They refused. The deadlock contributed to the Rockets' elimination before the playoffs, the star rejoined the team at the beginning of the promising 1992–93 season.

Houston won game after game that season. Finishing second in the Western Conference at the end of the regular season, the Rockets went to a seventh game in the Conference Semifinals against Seattle. But the SuperSonics won 103–100 in the final game.

The Rockets thrived under Rudy Tomjanovich and his emphasis on teamwork; but Hakeem Olajuwon attributed the team's sudden turnaround, which led to two championships and one MVP award, to his unshakable faith in Allah. Olajuwon strictly follows the laws of the Koran, even complying with Ramadan (the traditional fasting period), regardless of the strain it puts on his game.

In 1994, this faith combined with the team's talent brought the Rockets the NBA title following a 90–84 victory in the seventh and final game against the New York Knicks. Olajuwon was named MVP, with 26.9 points and 9.1 rebounds. He

READY FOR TAKE-OFF

*Olajuwon was the NBA leader in rebounds before giving
the Rockets the title in 1994 and 1995.*

also blocked 3.9 shots, including one that kept John Starks from scoring the game point that would have won the Knicks the title in the sixth game.

Rudy Tomjanovich joked that their strategy was simply to give the ball to "The Dream" and wait to see what he'd do with it. What Olajuwon did with the team was legendary. The Knicks' Dereck Harper said, "We could have stopped the rest of the team, but not Olajuwon."

Hakeem's parents came to Houston to watch their son play for the first time. "As they watched me, they realized how hard the job was and they said, 'you're working so hard, you deserve the money!'" recalls Hakeem. They were proud to have crossed the ocean to attend Hakeem's coronation.

The next season was a bit duller, or so people thought. At the end of the regular season, the Rockets finished sixth in the Western Conference. No one dared predict another championship and a new ring. But they were mistaken. Olajuwon was very weak in February (following Ramadan) but went to the playoffs in very good shape. Furthermore, his buddy Clyde Drexler replaced

THE DUEL
Olajuwon against O'Neal,
the two ruling forwards of the nineties.

Otis Thorpe in February. The trade was heavily criticized, but fans of the old Phi Slamma Jamma were happy—and with good reason.

Although away from home, the Rockets were able to eliminate the Utah Jazz, winning the fifth and final game 95–91 in Salt Lake City. In the next round, they played even better, edging out the Phoenix Suns in the seventh game 115–114. In the Conference Finals, the San Antonio Spurs went down four games to two. Now Houston would face Shaquille O'Neal, "Shaq," and the Orlando Magic in a memorable series final. Houston swept 4–0, and Olajuwon was named Finals MVP again with almost the same statistics as O'Neal: 32.7 points and 11.5 rebounds for Olajuwon; 28 points and 12.5 rebounds for Shaq. But Houston had become "The Dream's team." Even O'Neal, who received much more press, said humbly that Olajuwon was the best. But Hakeem didn't care about his popularity. He was a sage and a leader. As proof, he was placed on Dream Team III. Even though he had already played with the Nigerian team, basketball's international governing body declared him eligible to play with the U.S. national team. But as Hakeem put it, "Basketball is about humility; don't ever forget it."

"The Shaq"

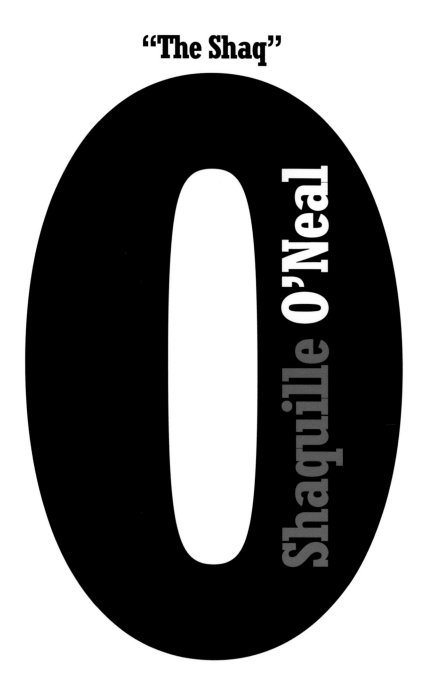

0

Shaquille O'Neal

Legend has it that when Dale Brown, coach of Louisiana State University, went to Germany in 1985 to attend a clinic, he came across a skinny 6'7" boy on the military base at Wilflecken. When Brown asked the boy if he'd been in the army long, he replied,—"I'm not in the army. I'm only thirteen years old." Dale Brown was startled and asked, "Where's your father, son?"—"Over there, sir." That's how the story began. The boy was named Shaquille O'Neal, and a couple of years later he would become one of the stars of the NBA in the closing days of a century that was both the generator and the victim of excess—something like Shaquille himself. His fans call him the best center of his generation. His critics say he's just a product of marketing. But Jordan has said that "he's someone the NBA needs." And he is extraordinary.

Shaquille O'Neal was born in Newark, New Jersey, on March 6, 1972. O'Neal's father, Joe Toney, left when his mother discovered she was pregnant. Philip Harrison, a municipal employee, fell in love with Lucille O'Neal, married her, and accepted the chubby-cheeked baby, whose name means "Little Warrior." This was the beginning of a much-talked-about childhood. Philip Harrison enlisted in the army, dragging his family from one city to the next, from base to base; first New Jersey, then Georgia, Texas, Germany, and finally back to New Jersey. Shaquille admitted he was a troublemaker who did everything except commit murder and do drugs; he stole, lied, cheated, broke car windows to take tapes and books, and so on. O'Neal kept busy from one end of the country to the other, despite the severe discipline of his step-father, Sergeant Harrison, who sometimes administered a beating. Shaquille was looking for attention—of any kind.

One day, when out with his street gang, the Warriors, he beat up a classmate who had squealed on him. The boy had an epileptic fit, and only the intervention of

SHAQUILLE O'NEAL/THE SHAQ
Born on March 6, 1972 in Newark, New Jersey/7'1" 300 lbs/High School: Cole High School, San Antonio, Texas/College: Louisiana State University/Selected by the Orlando Magic in 1992 (first overall pick)/Rookie of the Year in 1993/Leader in points scored, 1995/Four All-Star Game appearances/Member of Dream Teams II and III

a passer-by saved O'Neal from swallowing his own tongue. O'Neal got the scare of his life, as well as an unforgettable lesson. "After that, I calmed down," he said. "I told myself I had to change."

Harrison's transfer to Germany did the trick, but the culture shock was not easy. Shaquille started off playing soccer, but growth-related knee problems stopped him from progressing in the sport. His father suggested he turn to basketball, and Shaquille gave it a whirl, but didn't take it seriously. The teenager that Dale Brown met, despite being 6'7", couldn't even dunk. He still had a lot to learn. But at the time, Shaq only had one thing on his mind: getting out of a country where it was hard to find a Whopper or a Coke.

Shaquille had two years of high school to finish when he returned to the U.S. and attended Robert G. Cole High School in San Antonio, Texas, along with other children of enlisted personnel at the Fort Sam Houston army base. He and his father promised Dale Brown that he would go to Louisiana State for college, and until that time he was going to practice the basics. There was a lot of work to be done and O'Neal gave it his all. From afar, Brown made him work on jumping and getting into shape. One morning, a classmate taunted, "You're only good for the army, like your father." O'Neal redoubled his efforts, supervised by his father, who sometimes went to practices.

O'Neal's high school team started to annihilate everything in their path. O'Neal bent his first backboard and led Cole to a 68–1 record in two years. The only slip-up came against Liberty Hall after a long night of partying for O'Neal. He was on automatic pilot and committed four fouls in two minutes. His average of 32.1 points, 22 rebounds, and 8 blocked shots during his senior year fueled the interest of colleges across the nation. O'Neal could go anywhere, but he had made a promise to Dale Brown. Besides, Brown was the first to tell him what he really wanted to hear. He presented Shaq with a challenge, and Shaq wasn't going to pass it up.

O'Neal left for Louisiana State University in the fall of 1989. He was now 7'0" tall and intended to dominate the NCAA. He was a gift from heaven for the Tigers. But, despite his talent, he still had a lot of work to do. Robert Horry of the Houston Rockets remembers playing against him in college when he was just a freshman. He describes Shaq as a big kid who didn't know how to do anything. Brown said Shaq just wanted to be on defense and block a lot of shots. He didn't have a jump shot or a sky hook—but he had a great attitude. Brown tried to use Abdul-Jabbar, Walton, and Erving as inspiration.

In his first year, O'Neal was upstaged in the press by teammates Chris Jackson and Stanley Roberts, which shattered his ego. Both O'Neal and Roberts, who played at about the same level and had the same build, got in each other's way in the lane, and as a result LSU was eliminated in the second round of the NCAA tournament by Georgia Tech. Louisiana sang the blues. It was a similar story the following year. O'Neal didn't have any more excuses, because Roberts, having been declared "academically ineligible," couldn't play with the Tigers. In

EVENING WEAR (p. 70)
Shaq is a showman. He can do what ever he wants.
THE INTIMIDATOR (below)
No one can stop him from dunking.

addition, Jackson headed off to pursue the NBA dream, which left LSU completely in the hands of O'Neal. It was an especially difficult task, because O'Neal frequently had to deal with two or three big guards on his back who could only stop him by pulling on his arms. The referees pretended not to notice. "They didn't know how to whistle," explained O'Neal. "They thought that since I was so big and strong, I could handle all the blows and fouls on me." The fact that opponents were let loose on O'Neal didn't stop him from busting stats and Plexiglas in the same swoop: he scored an average of 27.6 points, 14.7 rebounds, and 5 blocks during his second year; and in his third year, he averaged 23.6 points, 14.1 rebounds, and 5 blocks. "He's a monster," exclaimed Magic Johnson. "He's the reincarnation of Wilt," added Wilt Chamberlain himself. "Shaq fever" hit the nation.

The newspapers talked only of "Shaq," and his TV appearances became more and more frequent. The country was enamoured of this 7'1", three-hundred-pound wonder with the face of an angel. Even so, Shaquille O'Neal couldn't win the championship title. Although he was first in rebounds in 1991 and leader in blocked shots in 1992, LSU choked every year come tournament time. So O'Neal cut out of school early and made himself eligible for the 1992 draft at the end of his junior year. Orlando struck gold and so did Shaq, who signed a juicy contract for forty million dollars over seven years—unprecedented for a rookie. It was an investment for the Magic, who believed they had the center of the future, a player who could run with the ball, dribble, and hustle like a guard. The Orlando arena was sold out for its first game, and Shaq slammed home 12 points against Miami and snatched 18 rebounds. The statistics were promising. He followed with 22 points and 15 rebounds against Washington, then with 35 points and 13 rebounds against Charlotte, and finally with 31 points and 21 rebounds against Washington again. O'Neal was the first rookie in history to be named NBA Player of the Week after only eight days in the NBA. Horace Grant, who played with Chicago, remembered his first collision. "I suddenly found myself against a wall. I thought there had been an earthquake." O'Neal didn't bother going around an opponent, instead he headed straight for him, like a tank. One night, after breaking the Net's backboard, he boasted, "Of course I did it on purpose.

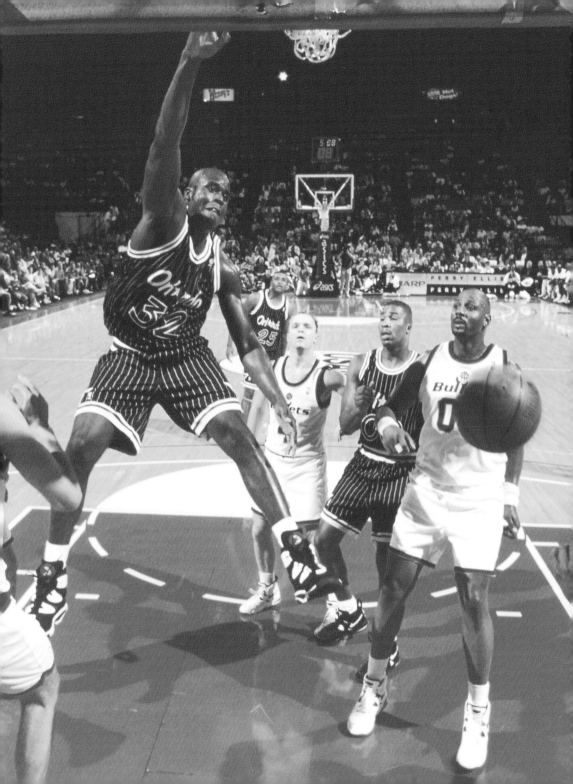

That way the guy in front of me is practically going to apologize for being there the next time." Before O'Neal, Orlando fans would be in the nose-bleed section during an away game. Now they turned up in the second row.

O'Neal soon signed a contract with Reebok for twenty million dollars and with Pepsi for twelve million dollars, both over a span of five years. He also signed with Spalding for six million dollars over four years, and with Classic Cards for more than two million dollars over two years. O'Neal released a rap album entitled *Shaq Diesel*. One of the cuts went to the nation's top fifteen. He also acted in the movie *Blue Chips*, after which he published his autobiography, *Shaq Attack*. Still, although he was drowning in money and glory, he was lacking in basketball titles. Shaquille O'Neal had finished his first season as Rookie of the Year, a reward for averaging 23.4 points, 13.9 rebounds, and 3.5 blocks, but Orlando had failed to make it to the playoffs. Tom Boswell of the *Washington Post* warned that basketball was about winning games, not beating the record for most appearances in commercials. 1994 bore the same fruit. For the second year in a row, O'Neal was the only NBA player to be in the top ten for points, rebounds, and field goal percentage, but Orlando, armed with Hardaway this time, was swept away 3–0 in the first round of the playoffs by Indiana. In 1995, O'Neal led the NBA in points, averaging 29.3, but the Magic, who made it to the finals, were too weak for Houston. The Rockets swept the series 4–0—another insult. After the final game, David Stern told Shaq, "We'll see you again." But when? The following year, it was Jordan and the Bulls who humiliated the Magic in the Conference Finals, 4–0. Dennis Rodman scoffed, "O'Neal has gotten way too much money too fast. He's not hungry to win."

LEAVE HIM ALONE! (left)
Shaquille O'Neal half-answers the media's questions in the Orlando locker room. Besides Jordan, he's the most publicized player of the NBA.
CALIFORNIA DREAMING (following double-page)
On July 18, 1996, O'Neal signs the biggest contract in the history of basketball with the Los Angeles Lakers: 123 million dollars for seven years!
THE STAR'S SIGNATURE (pp. 82–83)
Size 22.

On July 18, 1996, Shaq decided to sign with the Los Angeles Lakers for seven years and one hundred and twenty-three million dollars. It was the biggest contract ever signed in the history of the game. He said that when he was little, he was fascinated by Magic and Kareem. Hollywood also intrigued him—California dreaming. But the first year did not end in a title. O'Neal damaged his knee (partially tearing a ligament) and had to let his team fend for itself for two whole months. In the playoffs, the Jazz beat the Lakers (3–1). A temporary setback.

Many criticize O'Neal's unpolished technique, his mediocre free-throwing, his lack of mobility, his impertinence, and his desire for a media image. However, O'Neal is still young. It took Jordan seven years to get his first championship title. Dale Brown knew Shaquille would perhaps be a very great player, but for the moment, Shaq needs to continue to work hard. Americans know it: "For the present, he is still the future…"

Larry B**bird**

"I leave the game I love"

On February 4, 1993, 15,000 people jammed the stands of the old Boston Garden to pay respect to a legend. On the floor, the thirty-six-year-old Larry Bird, alongside his wife Dinah and little boy Connor, hoisted up his number "33" Celtic jersey with care. It was an unforgettable sight, one that symbolized the end of an era that basketball fans had followed with devotion.

It all began on December 7, 1956, with the birth of Larry in West Baden, a tiny town in the heart of Indiana. His mother Georgia was a waitress in a bar and his father restored furniture. Larry was thirteen when his family moved a few miles away to French Lick, a town with a population of 2,500. There was nothing for Larry Bird in French Lick except basketball, and he quietly built his reputation in the area. He was the leader of the Spring Valley High School basketball team, and people from all around had heard about him.

Bobby Knight, the famous coach at Indiana University, set off to convince Larry to come to the Bloomington campus, a college basketball sanctuary. Larry went to check it out, but returned terrified. For the kid from French Lick, Bloomington was overwhelming, a sprawling campus where close to 80,000 students gathered every day. He backed out only to face a hellish year back home. Upon his return home, his father committed suicide, and Larry suddenly found himself shouldering much of the subsequent family responsibility. When Indiana State recruited him, he embraced the opportunity.

LARRY BIRD
Born on December 7, 1956 in West Baden, Indiana/6'8" 234 lbs/High School: Springs Valley High School, Indiana/College: Indiana State/Picked by the Boston Celtics in the first round (sixth overall pick) in 1978/Rookie of the Year in 1980/Wins the NBA championships with the Celtics in 1981, 1984 and 1986/Regular season MVP in 1984, 1985 and 1986/Finals MVP in 1984 and 1986/Leader in free throws in 1984, 1986, 1987 and 1990/All-NBA First Team in 1980, 1981, 1982, 1983, 1984, 1985, 1986, 1987 and 1988/Twelve All-Star Game appearances; MVP in 1982/Winner of the Long-Distance Shootout in 1986, 1987 and 1988/Member of Dream Team I

Bird started at Indiana State in the fall of 1975. The school, with only 10,000 students, was more his size. In the coming months, Bird would endure a number of changes. Although he was only nineteen, he was facing a divorce. During the divorce proceedings, his wife informed him that she was pregnant. Despite his troubled personal life, Bird was at the peak of his form on the court. His stat sheet read a remarkable average of 32.8 points and 13.3 rebounds at the end of the season. He finished 1979 with flying colors, qualifying for the Final Four in Salt Lake City, and winning the semifinals against De Paul. In the finals, he was going to face Michigan State—and Magic Johnson.

Few people realized that they were watching the two players that would mark the eighties by revolutionizing the NBA. The pair seemed to have nothing in common: one was white, the other black; one was shy, reserved, his mouth closed to the media, and the other open, spontaneous, the champion of grand statements; one played forward, the other point guard; one would play in the old, predominantly white city of Boston, while the other would play in the wildly diverse city of Los Angeles.

On March 26, 1979, at the Special Events Center in Salt Lake City, the game turned to Magic's advantage. Michigan State won 75–64. Bird was devastated. Nevertheless, the NBA was waiting for him—Boston wanted him, no matter what the cost.

After a long period of success, the Celtics found themselves at the bottom of the standings. In November 1979, Red Auerbach, the head of the franchise, offered Bird more than six hundred thousand dollars over five years. Even though the rookie said he would have begged to be on the team, he followed the negotiations closely. Money is money. The Celtics ended up with one of the best deals in their history.

Immediately, Bird propelled the Celtics into the Conference Finals. He filled the Garden and was elected Rookie of the Year. The following season, along with Robert Parish and Kevin McHale, he led his team to the title with a 4–2 win over Houston. This started the Bird trilogies: three championship titles (1981, 1984, and 1986) and three NBA MVP awards (1984, 1985, and 1986), against two lost finals (1985 and 1987). Magic Johnson praised Bird as the ultimate player, as a man who could turn his teammates into stars.

On the court, Bird could do almost everything better than the others. He knew where to go, how to pass, how to shoot, and most of all, he had a feel for the game. He was like a computer that constantly anticipated the next move. He is one of a very small group of players to accumulate a career total of more than 20,000 points, 5,000 rebounds, and 5,000 assists.

Bird didn't talk to the press. Bill Hodges, his coach at Indiana State, said he'd never seen anyone so contained. He was a bit more talkative with his opponents though. In fact, before the Long-Distance Shootout at the 1986 All-Star Game, he taunted, "So guys, who'll come in second today?" He won the contest three years in a row.

In 1988, Bird re-signed with the Celtics for six million dollars a year, but the team's golden age was coming to an end. The team was aging, and Larry's back problems were worsening. Bird played in agony and had to wear a back brace; he spent half-times on the massage table. In 1989, he had his first operation.

In 1992, he spent most of his games with the Dream Team stretched out on his back on the floor in front of the bench. Nevertheless, he managed to score the first two baskets of the team's history, against Cuba. "I absolutely had to get them," he said. "That way, if I didn't score anymore during the tournament, I could say that I got the first two!"

On February 4, 1993, Bird retired. The Celtics lost their soul. Oddly enough, the man was never graced with any kind of nickname, with the brief exception of "Kodak," coined by his early 1980s coach Bill Fitch. Perhaps it's an *a posteriori* way of immortalizing the big white guy, one of the best all-around players of the century. He's up there at the top with his friend Magic Johnson, close by his side, as always.

BIRD HAD OVERWHELMED THE NATION. HIS RETIREMENT MARKED THE END OF AN ERA

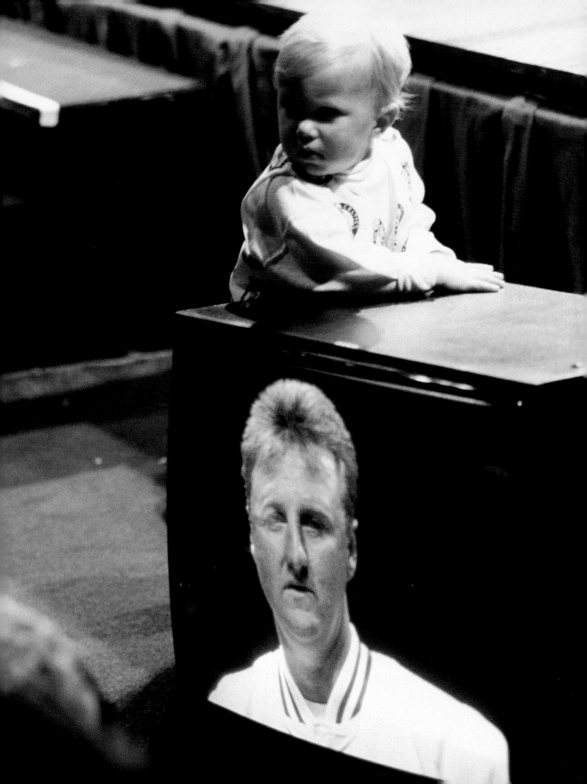

LARRY...THANK Y[
13 GREAT SEA[

P

Scottie Pippen

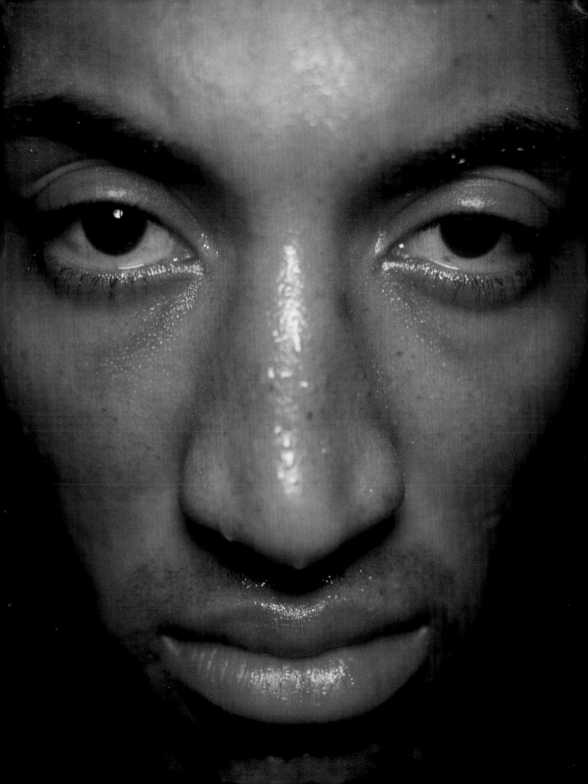

In 1987, when Bulls general manager Jerry Krause told Michael Jordan that he intended to choose a certain Scottie Pippen in the next draft, Jordan looked at him in disbelief: "Who?"—"Scottie Pippen, of Central Arkansas, an NAIA college."—"There are people interested in what's going on in those schools?" Jerry Krause chuckled, "Yeah, me." The conversation is only slightly romanticized.

Scottie Pippen is an NBA miracle. Only four years before his first championship title with the Bulls, he was unknown to the scouts. There was certainly no money put down on his future. But Krause had foresight and included Pippen in his plan to build one of the greatest teams of all time. Bulls' coach Phil Jackson noted that Pippen's personal development coincided with the team's coming to power. Today, Scottie Pippen can look at where he came from—his small town, his small high school and college—and say to himself that this Southern boy has come a very long way.

Imagine Hamburg, Arkansas, a town with a population of 3,500, about ten miles from Louisiana. Ethel and Preston Pippen were constantly trying to make ends meet in order to support their family. He worked in the Georgia Pacific paper mill, and she stayed at home to take care of the family. Scottie was born on September 25, 1965, the youngest of twelve children.

At school, he was the laughing-stock of the basketball team because he was shorter than the others. The coach didn't want to be bothered with him. Pippen was also too small for football, and wound up taking care of the uniforms. Yet he was happy just to be around the players. When Scottie was fifteen, his father

SCOTTIE PIPPEN
Born on September 25, 1965 in Hamburg, Arkansas/6'7" 228 lbs/High School: Hamburg High School, Arkansas/College: University of Central Arkansas/ Drafted by the Seattle SuperSonics in the first round (fifth overall pick)/Wins NBA championship with the Chicago Bulls in 1991, 1992, 1993, 1996 and 1997/Member of the All-Defensive First Team in 1992, 1993, 1994, 1995, 1996 and 1997/All-NBA First Team in 1994, 1995, 1996/Seven All-Star Game appearances; MVP in 1994/Member of Dream Teams I and III

suffered a ruptured blood vessel in his brain that left him unable to speak and bound to a wheelchair for the rest of his life. These early days were difficult, but Pippen said it made him grow up fast—in every way. By his senior year, Pippen was 5'11", and his basketball coach, Donald Wayne, finally agreed to let him play for a couple of minutes to make him happy.

No college really wanted him after high school. It was Donald Wayne again who did him a favor, recommending him to his friend Don Dyer, coach at Central Arkansas. There, Pippen continued to pick up balls, sweep the floor, and wash uniforms, but he also got some playing time, averaging 4.3 points and 2.9 rebounds. Pippen admitted that he was nothing at first. But he continued to grow, and was 6'5" by his sophomore year. Having practiced all summer, and built up some muscle, he now intended to gain some respect. During the year, he averaged 18.5 points and snatched 9.2 rebounds—a total metamorphosis. It was at this point that he realized the NBA was a possibility.

Recruiters didn't take Pippen's stats very seriously because he came from the NAIA. But his pre-draft performance proved them wrong. The Bulls' Jerry Krause had spotted Pippen very early on, but he could no longer keep him from the attention of other teams. So he started wheeling and dealing. Krause knew that Sacramento, who had the sixth draft pick, wanted Pippen. Chicago picked eighth, so Krause got in touch with Seattle, who had the fifth overall pick, and struck a deal: the SuperSonics would select Pippen, then trade him to the Bulls for Olden Polynice and future draft considerations. This was where the real story began.

In 1988, Michael Jordan *was* the Bulls. A disciplined Pippen immediately came to his aid, making the Bulls the team of the 1990s. With multidimensional talents, this 6'7" forward could also act as a point guard, shooter, and power forward; his talent was both uncommon and invaluable. It took time, however, for Pippen to reach his prime. His first year was a disaster. In addition to averaging only 7.9 points and 3.8 rebounds, he developed back problems by the end of the season. His operation during the summer was a blow to his spirits, and he worried that his career was over. But it was only beginning. As of spring 1989, he improved every week and climbed to 14.4 points, 6.1 rebounds, and 3.5 assists per game.

The Bulls' new coach, Phil Jackson, helped him grow even stronger. Suddenly, there was another player on the team—someone in addition to Jordan—who could charge the basket and deliver reliable assists. Pippen took some of the pressure off of Jordan. Opponents now had two players to stop. Pippen finished the season with 16.5 points and 6.7 rebounds per game. The Bulls gained another dimension, and it was no surprise that they were champions three years in a row in 1991, 1992, and 1993. Many considered Pippen the best all-around player in the NBA as well as a future MVP candidate. But Jordan overshadowed him, and Pippen had a hard time with it.

ONE OF THE NBA'S POWERHOUSES (pp. 100–101)
Michael Jordan sees the Bulls as Pippen's team.
THE FOURTH DIMENSION (pp. 104–105)
A multidimensional player, Pippen shines in all categories.
He's the most complete player in the league.
PIPPEN, ALL-STAR GAME MVP 1994 (p. 111)
With Jordan gone, he tries to become "The Man."

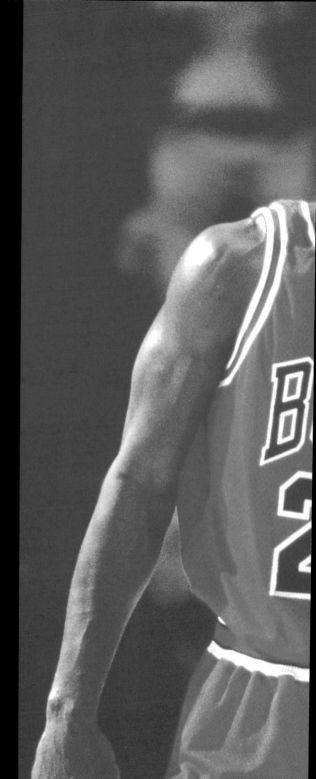

Pippen needs Jordan to shine and vice-versa. The proof? Jordan says he wouldn't have come back if Scottie had been traded for Kemp. No one can replace Pippen.

When Jordan left in 1993, Pippen had the chance to become "the man" around whom Chicago could build its future. "I've got to show the way," said Pippen—but he didn't quite fit the part. Pippen liked to blame Jerry Krause for bringing in Toni Kukoc for 3.5 million dollars a year. Pippen who made "only" 2.9 million dollars a year, felt disrespected and swindled. He snapped in the third game of the playoffs against New York. The Knicks were leading by two points with one minute eight seconds left in the game, but Pippen refused to play because Phil Jackson had ordered that the final shot be given to Kukoc. "Are you in or out?" yelled Jackson. "Out!" Pippen was enraged. Kukoc ended up leading the Bulls to the win, and Krause ended up wanting to trade Pippen for Shawn Kemp. Without Michael Jordan, the team fell apart. Only a month earlier, Pippen was named All-Star MVP in Minneapolis. But even though his stats were up (22 points, 8.7 rebounds, and 5.6 passes), he knew he didn't have what it took to score 30 or 40 points per game and save the team like Jordan had. To shine, Pippen needed Jordan, and vice-versa. Jordan said that he wouldn't have come back if Pippen had been traded for Kemp, because no one was worth Pippen. The Bulls were Pippen's team, and Jordan wasn't just being diplomatic. He was the boss in the locker room, and Pippen was the boss on the court. Things eventually calmed down, and Chicago found its balance again, landing the title in 1996. It was the same in 1997. "The MVP trophy is for me and the automobile that goes with it is for him," hooted Jordan just after his fifth title. The two men embraced each other. The kid from Arkansas wasn't at the end of the line. His journey continues.

B

Charles Barkley

"Sir Charles"

Everyone knows Charles Barkley has a big mouth. He is hated—but he is also loved. "Sir Charles" knows his time in basketball is almost over. Soon, he'll be paralyzed with pain, limping around like "a cripple," says Barkley, his body exhausted and injury-ridden. He's been talking about retirement since he collapsed in the Phoenix Suns' training camp. Tests showed that he had serious disc problems. His incredible pain took him out for part of the 1993–94 and 1994–95 seasons. But he swears he's doing better since then, and that as long as he can play, and play well, he'll do so. As proof, he was chosen for the Atlanta Games at the last minute, like Mitch Richmond. "Sir Charles" had become one of the best ambassadors of the NBA, a role model, even if he plays it down. "Guys, I'm just a basketball player!"

Charles Barkley was born on February 20, 1963, in Leeds, Alabama, a town of 8,000. His father left the family when Barkley was a year old, and it was his mother and grandmother who raised him. His grandmother was particularly influential since his mom was often out working to support the family. She earned barely enough to support the children.

Barkley's grandmother taught him religious values and an important lesson: "Listen to your heart. Know how you feel." Barkley would remember this. As a teenager, he attended Leeds High School, where he spent most of his time in the playground trying to prove that he was as good a basketball player as the others, even though he was only 5'9". He was teased a lot, since his "baby fat" hadn't turned to muscle yet. Although he worked hard, it was really a fluke that he ended up at Auburn University. He had persuaded the recruiter to choose him over his teammate.

CHARLES BARKLEY/SIR CHARLES
Born on February 20, 1963 in Leeds, Alabama/6'6" 252 lbs/High School: Leeds High School, Alabama/College: Auburn University/Picked fifth in the first round of the draft by the Philadelphia 76ers/Leader in rebounds in 1987/League MVP in 1993/All-NBA First Team in 1988, 1989, 1990, 1991 and 1993/Ten NBA All-Star Game appearances; MVP in 1991/Member of Dream Teams I and III

Auburn was Bo Jackson's college, and the whole school centered around football. Close to 80,000 fans attended the football games, while only 3,000–4,000 fans straggled into the basketball games. But things changed when Barkley came along. The big guy (he now weighed 265 pounds and was 6'5") put on a good show. His team won, and he became one of the best players in the Southeastern Conference. The fans responded. During these early games, Barkley stuffed himself with pizza. "It's annoying," he says today, "that's all people remember about that period."

In 1984, after three years of college, he decided to attempt the NBA. Barkley, a highly rated player, was sought by the Philadelphia 76ers, the 1983 champions, with Julius Erving and Moses Malone in their ranks. What's more, Bobby Knight, who was in charge of making up the American team for the Los Angeles Olympic Games, called him up for the trials. "One thing," he said, "you have to lose forty-five pounds."

The trials were not successful. Knight had to remind Barkley over and over again that he was the boss. In the end, both Barkley and Stockton were cut from the team. Knight, flanked by two assistants and almost twenty coaches to supervise the team, kept Jordan, Ewing, and Mullin as their core players. Even without Barkley and Stockton, however, the United States would beat Spain by more than 30 points in the final game for the gold.

Philadelphia 76ers owner Harold Katz warned Barkley in June that if he wanted to be signed, he'd have to weigh in at under 275 lbs. But with two days to go until the draft, the scale still read more than 287 lbs. When the time came for the 76ers to choose, however, they announced, "and as the fifth pick, the Sixers choose… Charles Barkley." Harold Katz and the 76ers management couldn't pass up the star; regardless of Erving's and Malone's wizardry, the team was getting old and needed new blood. Change was essential.

At first, Barkley was Moses Malone's victim, but not for long. Barkley quickly became one of the best players in the NBA: he led in rebounds in 1987, averaging 14.6 per game. Never before had a player as short as Barkley been first in rebounds. He brought new life to the Spectrum. Although the team could have done better, the show was always great. One day, Barkley moved the backboard

a couple of inches when dunking a bit too hard. One of the security guards commented, "The last time that we moved the backboard like that, we had to use a fork lift!"

In 1991, Barkley was selected MVP of the All-Star Game. Only three days before, he had played with the 76ers, but nevertheless had announced his withdrawal from the All-Star Game on account of an injury. The NBA wouldn't allow his withdrawal and threatened to suspend him. So Barkley played. The result: 22 points, 17 rebounds, and 4 assists, and an MVP title. All the while, Barkley continued to shower journalists with his killer sound bytes. "We don't need referees, but the white guys need the work. All the players are black." The NBA wasn't impressed.

Meanwhile, although "Sir Charles" was able to pick up some awards here and there, he was missing the ultimate one: the championship title and the ring. Philadelphia was out of the running. Meanwhile, Barkley destroyed his relationship with his managers. He was fined thousands of dollars by the NBA and didn't hesitate to criticize everyone in his autobiography, appropriately titled *Outrageous*. Two bar brawls in Milwaukee and Chicago made matters worse.

On June 17, 1992, Barkley was traded to the Phoenix Suns for Jeff Hornacek, Tim Perry, and Andrew Lang. He was off to a new adventure and a new life. The Suns had renewed ambitions, and were changing their coach, their logo, and their stadium, all in the same year. It was a lot, but it worked. After a summer of gold with the Dream Team (Barkley was named MVP), he played a dream season: the Suns won 62 games, lost only 20, and charged straight to the finals against the Bulls. The final pitted Barkley against his buddy Jordan. The Suns, with the better record, started with the home-court advantage, but nothing went as planned. The Bulls won the first two games in the series before heading off to their stadium for the next three games. Chicago wanted one thing: to see their Bulls win the title at home.

The Suns succeeded in getting back into the series at three games to two. In the fifth game, Barkley tormented the Bulls' bench, "Hey, guys, I have tickets for Sunday if you need them." Sunday, they were to head back to Phoenix for a game to remember. The Suns were moments away from tying the series at three games apiece, when John Paxson ruined their chances, scoring a three-pointer with 3.9 seconds to go in the game. The Bulls won. Barkley was crushed. Despite his 27.3 points and 13 rebounds average in the finals, despite being MVP of the regular season, he knew that his last chance at winning an NBA title had just slipped through his fingers. Nevertheless, in 1996, he signed with Houston to try and wrest this highly coveted title, playing with Olajuwon and Drexler, two other league giants. Despite their formidable team, the Rockets lost to the Jazz in the Conference Finals (4–2).

Barkley definitely has opinions. He doesn't want to be a role model for inner-city kids. He thinks children's parents are the ones who should be the

BAD REPUTATION (below)
The refs are among his favorite targets, but the press loves his killer statements. From 1987 to 1996 he's named nine times to the All-Interview First Team, the best at the mic.
LAST ONE OUT (pp. 122–123)
Regardless of the all the blows, regardless of his weary body, Barkley's smile shows a man who loves the game too much to just leave it.

role models. Why should playing basketball make someone a substitute, a teacher of children's morals? When Barkley was a child, Superman and Batman were his idols. Although he loved to watch Dr. J and Magic play, they weren't his heroes.

Many scoff at his political beliefs but Barkley ignores his critics. He has donated a lot of time and money to charity. Barkley knows that basketball, with all its extravagances, is only a game for him; real life is elsewhere. It's a place where you let your emotions out, where you "listen to your heart," just like his grandmother taught him.

While Barkley is certainly a trouble-maker, he's often provoked. He wants to live like a normal guy and be left alone. His mood swings made him an outcast in Philly. In 1992, he left the 76ers to join the Suns.

R

Dennis Rodman

"The Worm"

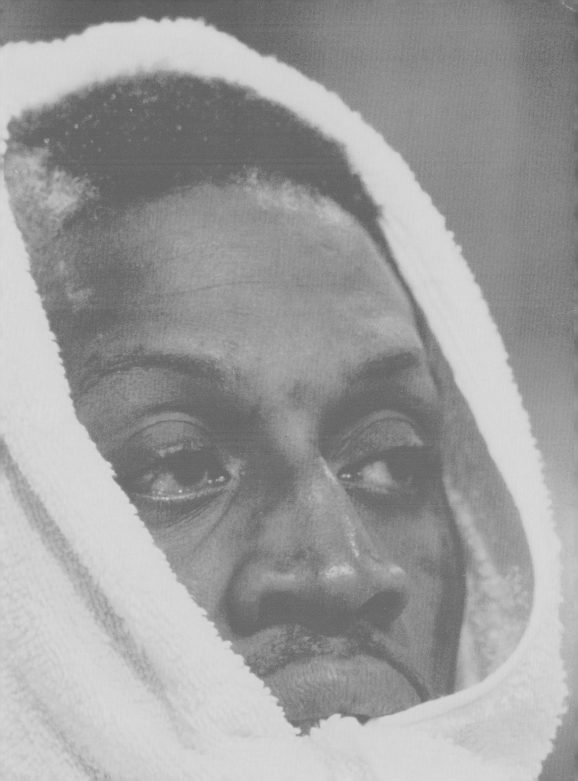

Dennis Rodman is the ugly duckling of the NBA. The first things anyone will tell you about him are: one, he slept with Madonna; two, he has a bunch of tattoos, wears earrings, pierces his body, and dyes his hair bright red or fluorescent green, depending on his mood; and three, he's an extraordinary player. Perhaps the picture's a bit too simple.

Rodman has a fiery temper. He's a trouble-maker. Basketball has done a lot for him, but he hates the game's environment. He doesn't care if the league disapproves of him. All he wants is to be master of his destiny. Rodman isn't calculating. He gives his all, both on and off the court. However, he's a constant slap-in-the-face to conventional America. Bulls general manager Jerry Krause is not concerned with Rodman's hair color. He hired him to capture the title and Rodman's done his job.

Dennis Keith Rodman was born on May 13, 1961, in Trenton, New Jersey. When Rodman was three years old, his father enlisted in the Air Force and left town, leaving Rodman's mother, Shirley, alone to raise her son and two daughters, Debra and Kim. As a child, Dennis didn't like basketball. His two sisters, good high school players themselves, tried to interest him in the sport, but he preferred the aerial bombs of the Dallas Cowboys, the football team from their new hometown. In high school, Rodman gave basketball a whirl, but without success. As a teenager, Rodman did odd jobs to earn a little money. At one point, he did maintenance work at the Dallas airport. But one day he was arrested for stealing watches and spent the night at the police station. His mother kicked him out of the house. "I found myself homeless for six months when I was only nineteen,"

DENNIS RODMAN/THE WORM
Born on May 13, 1961 in Trenton, New Jersey/6'8" 220 lbs/High School: South Oak Cliff High School, Dallas, Texas/College: Southern Oklahoma State/Selected in the second round by the Detroit Pistons (twenty-seventh overall pick)/Wins the NBA championship with the Detroit Pistons in 1989 and 1990, and with the Chicago Bulls in 1996 and 1997/Defensive Player of the Year 1990 and 1991/League leader in rebounds in 1992, 1993, 1994, 1995, 1996 and 1997/All-Defensive First Team in 1989, 1990, 1991, 1992, 1993 and 1996/Two All-Star Game appearances

he recalls. "I was still living in Dallas, but I wasn't going to school anymore and I wasn't doing anything with my life. I spent my time talking with my friends and I slept on the sidewalk. Some nights, I wandered for hours, heading nowhere." It was a viscious circle. His sisters urged him to sign up for the Cooke County Junior College basketball training camp. He was kicked out after sixteen games. Luckily, Lonn Reismann spotted him. He was the coach at Southeastern Oklahoma State, a second-rate, soon-to-be NAIA college, who wanted Rodman at whatever the cost. "I don't know where he saw me play," said Rodman, "but he was convinced that I was the player his team was missing."

The change in Rodman's life was abrupt. He left Dallas immediately for Durant, a small town of 6,000. During pre-season training, he met Bryne Rich, a boy mourning the death of his best friend. Dennis helped him out. Bryne was 13 and Dennis was 22, but they were soon as close as brothers. The Richs lived on a farm in Bokchito, about 12 miles from Durant, and they became Rodman's adoptive family. Rodman remembers: "It was unreal: again and again I had confronted racism, and now I found myself there, living with a white family, waking up at five in the morning to milk the cows. Without them, I might not be here."

In 96 college games, Rodman logged an average of 25.7 points and grabbed 15.7 rebounds. Soon afterwards, Rodman, who was already 25 years old, saw his life head off in another direction for a second time. To everyone's surprise, he was chosen in the second round of the draft by the Detroit Pistons as the twenty-seventh overall pick.

During his first practice with the Pistons, a reporter approached Rodman and asked him who he was. Rodman looked at him and said, "Nobody, I've come from nowhere." Rodman hadn't played in high school or in the NCAA, but he quickly became a big player in the NBA. His job: defense. He knew he would never be a big scorer, and therefore concentrated on snatching all the rebounds he could. It was a good choice. Detroit soon developed the league's best defense. At the same time, Rodman exposed his volatile temper, becoming another one of the Bad Boys. After the Pistons lost to the Celtics in 1987, he blurted out that he thought Larry Bird was overrated and only got the attention he did because he's white. Only time and his subsequent success eradicated the slip. Coach

Chuck Daly took Rodman under his wing, like a father. Rodman de-throned Laimbeer as Detroit's leader in rebounds and was the best sixth man in the NBA in the 1988–89 campaign. The Detroit Pistons took the championship title that same year, and the emotional Rodman broke into tears during the celebratory parade.

The Pistons picked up the title again in 1993, and Rodman was selected Defensive Player of the Year in 1990 and 1991. In 1992, he led the NBA in rebounds for the first time with 18.7 per game—a phenomenal average.

Dennis Rodman, despite his height of 6'8", is there to get rebounds. He knows that 65 percent of them can be grabbed on the opposite side of the shooter and

THE WORM IS HOT (p. 132)

Dennis Rodman isn't only a great jumper. He can also wiggle in the air to snatch the ball. That's where he got his name.

A NOT SO SIMPLE PAST (p. 133)

Scottie Pippen hated him. The two almost go at it in 1991, before finding themselves on the same team four years later.

places himself accordingly. But, he also knows how to twist himself in mid-air to seize the ball—a contortion similar to his stance at the pinball machine. This is where he got the name, "The Worm." Phil Taylor wrote in *Sports Illustrated*, "Rodman turns the rebound into a science and at the same time makes it a whole new art."

His trade to San Antonio made him a star. First, he was "fashionably" late for the pre-season press conference because he was getting his hair done! Rodman's punk look gained him even more attention. He arrived late again and again, annoying both his teammates and coach. One day he missed the plane to Houston, and didn't show up until five minutes before the start of the game. He shrugged off the incident, but the coach benched him. After a few minutes, Rodman wrote, "I am sorry. Can I play please?" on a paper towel. "You can only love him," confessed his coach John Lucas, who excused all his idiosyncrasies, including the ritual of taking off his shoes in the middle of a game so he could feel fresh when he returned.

Rodman had a hard time with his divorce and the subsequent separation from his little girl, Alexis. His distress was evident, though he seemed to find comfort

DEMOLITION MAN (p. 135)
His bleached blonde hair and his performance on the court earn him this nickname in San Antonio. He keeps it in Chicago.
"HAIR" RODMAN (pp. 138–139)
Left, the desire to capture a third title with Detroit. Right, the red ribbon (in his hair) symbolizing the fight against AIDS, worn during the 1996 finals.

in the arms of Madonna, who sometimes dropped him off in her limo five minutes before the opening toss. The Spurs eventually replaced John Lucas with Bob Hill, a less forgiving coach. Hill reacted strongly after an ESPN interview in which Rodman said that teammate David Robinson didn't deserve eight or nine million dollars for not winning a title. Rodman is a winner, a fighter, and he couldn't stand to see the Spurs eliminated in the playoffs, even if they did put up a good fight. He grumbled that Robinson wasn't a leader, and insisted that "an MVP needs to move his butt a bit more in the playoffs." Bob Hill had had enough.

In 1995, San Antonio decided to trade Rodman, and the Bulls picked him up. Krause, the Bulls' general manager, reported that they spent 36 hours with Rodman before deciding to sign him. Rodman said he had come to play basketball and nothing else. The Bulls needed someone good in rebounding, and Rodman, whose 14.9 average equaled Moses Malone's record, was first in the category for the fifth consecutive time. He also helped bring the Bulls their fourth championship win, and received two votes to become

league MVP. (Jordan received six votes, Kemp three.)

After the finals, Rodman spontaneously announced, "I promised one thing to this city, and I kept my promise: to bring the title to Chicago. I acted as a perfect team member—except for when I changed outfits and dyed my hair. But now my mission is accomplished. And I want the referees to know one thing, and that's that I will never change. They can go fuck themselves."

During the 1996–97 season, Rodman, thanks to a sixth consecutive title as best leader in rebounds (16.1 per game), contributed to another Bulls triumph. But in January, Rodman was suspended for 11 games for kicking a camera operator; in June, he was fined $50,000 for making insensitive remarks about Mormons. Rodman sets *another* NBA record for outrageousness. He is, indeed, one of a kind.

Dangerous liaisons: the Madonna-Rodman fling is front-page news. At one point, the singer even considers buying the Chicago Bulls! Rodman becomes a rock star.

"I don't have a lot of respect for most of the players in the NBA, but I do for John." It was February 1, 1995. Magic Johnson's words were projected onto the giant screen that hangs over the floor of the Delta Center, and they got a rare smile out of John Stockton. The fans were on their feet cheering. A few minutes earlier, the Utah-Denver game was interrupted to observe the moment: Stockton's 9,922nd assist with the NBA, breaking Magic's record of 9,921. It was an historic moment, but Stockton was almost embarrassed about being put in the same league as the champion Magic Johnson. Stockton doesn't fancy himself a legend; he's just an ordinary American who likes to play basketball and then go home to his wife and kids. He's a quiet hero, a throw-back to a time when money wasn't a cardinal value on the court. He's from another world—a good guy.

John Stockton was born on March 26, 1962, in Spokane, Washington, not far from Seattle. His family has Irish roots and his father ran a pub close to the house. John still believes in his father's values of family and honesty. Protected by his family, John was free to let out his aggressiveness on the nearby court with his brother Steve, who was four years older and one of the best players in their high school. Steve was John's idol. On a nice day, the Stockton brothers could be seen emerging at daybreak to go to the gym or the playground.

John played a lot, but never thought about going pro. That was a dream for other people. He was clear-headed. He was only 5'5" at age fourteen, a handicap that prevented him from being a top player at the high school level, let alone college. He knew this from the start and decided that the only way to make a name for himself would be to dish the ball to the big guys on the team.

It was no surprise when he was not recruited by a single renowned university

JOHN STOCKTON
Born on March 26, 1962 in Spokane, Washington/6'1" 175 lbs/High School: Gonzaga Prep., Spokane/College: Gonzaga University/Drafted by the Utah Jazz in 1984 in the first round (sixteenth overall pick)/Leader in assists in 1988, 1989, 1990, 1991, 1992, 1993, 1994, 1995 and 1996/Leader in steals 1989 and 1992/All-NBA First Team in 1994 and 1995/Nine All-Star Game appearances; MVP in 1993/Member of Dream Teams I and III

after he graduated from high school. This didn't bother him, however, because he didn't really want to leave the area. Both his father and grandfather (a good football player) went to Gonzaga University, and John decided to follow in their footsteps. Gonzaga is a small, little-known Catholic university with a strong basketball program. Its proximity to his home was an added attraction—the family circle remained tight.

John fit right in as a Gonzaga Bulldog, even though it took a while for him to draw the attention of his opponents. He ended his first year averaging only 3.1 points, but then climbed to 11.2 points his second year. By the end of his junior year he averaged 13.9. He was starting to stand out. At 6'1", Stockton played a conventional game, but his moves and passes were surgically precise. He saw everything before everyone else, was good on defense, knew how to manage the ball, and could shoot well. By his senior year, he averaged 20.9 points, surpassing his brother Steve. Stockton became Gonzaga's star player, the first to score more than 1,000 points and make more than 500 assists. Dan Fitzgerald, athletic director, said that the school would have to wait another hundred years before they'd see something like him again.

After college, Stockton could start to think seriously about playing in the NBA, especially when Bobby Knight, in his quest to put together an American team for the Los Angeles Games, asked him to join the Olympic trials in Bloomington. Unfortunately, the trials did not go well. Stockton was the last one to be cut from the team. He later admitted that this was the biggest let-down of his life, and believed the opportunity would never come again. Bobby Knight never explained his decision, but it's clear that Stockton's height, just over six feet, might have worked against him. Stockton thought his height would keep him out of the 1984 NBA draft as well, but he was wrong. The Utah Jazz had spotted him and chose him with the sixteenth overall pick in the first round. He was off to Salt Lake City.

Stockton liked the clean, safe Mormon capital and its people. There was no pressure, and the place was safe from intense media attention. Still the new Jazz guard encountered a few problems concerning his salary, so he missed some of his pre-season training. When he arrived, Stockton was ready for his first practice. His teammates were amazed.

It would take three years before Stockton really stood out on the team and in the NBA. At first, the kid from Spokane was backup to the starting point guard Ricky Green and ranged between five and eight points and assists in twenty minutes of game time. But soon everything changed. His playing time increased, and the team acquired better players. Stockton modestly gave the credit for his own success to the excellent work of his teammates. In 1987–88, he led in assists for the first time, and established a new NBA record of 1,128 assists in eighty-two games. He would beat his own record twice and would also have the highest assist average nine seasons in a row, between 1986 and 1996. On February 1, 1995, Magic Johnson predicted across that giant screen at the Delta Center that no one like Stockton would ever be seen again. He was probably right. Jazz boss Frank Layden said Stockton is like Joe Montana—he'll give you a sharp pass if you want one, or a gentle pass, if you prefer. "In addition, he's got eyes in the

RELUCTANT HERO

On February 1st, 1995, John Stockton becomes the all-time leader in assists, beating the 9,921 assists handed out by Magic. His little girl is in his arms. "Don't compare me to him. He's a legend."

back of his head. No one is better." Two weeks later, on February 18, Stockton shot past the extraordinary 10,000 assist mark, and on February 20, he surpassed Maurice Cheeks' 2,310 steals to become the NBA's all-time leader in that category as well.

The humble Stockton says that Karl Malone makes his job easy. The two are a unit. For more than ten years, fans have watched the same set-up: Malone, back turned to the basket, at one end of the court. When Stockton gives him the ball, he turns and scores. Perhaps this is a simplistic description of two men who get

THE OTHER MAGICIAN (above and right)
His achievements are unmatched. From 1988 to 1996, Stockton is leader in assists nine times. Magic was leader in assists only four times in a row.
"THE RADAR" (p. 151)
His nickname. Jazz boss Frank Layden says, "He's got eyes in the back of his head. No one is better."

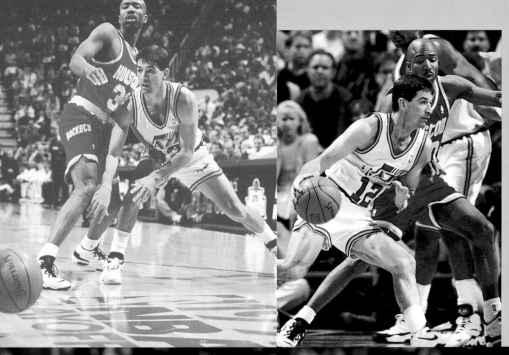

along perfectly, both on and off the court. Malone said he was surprised that people didn't consider Stockton the best guard in history, even though his stats prove he is. The two players are inseparable. During the 1993 All-Star Game, they were named co-MVPs. Stockton is self-conscious. Every now and then, however, Malone pushes him in front of the TV cameras. Stockton would never face them without Malone.

In 1997, Stockton and Malone took Utah to the finals for the first time, thanks to a three-pointer scored by Stockton with only a few seconds to go in the sixth game against Houston. Three weeks later, Jordan and the Bulls smashed the Jazz's dream. "We'll be back," say the indestructible Malone and Stockton. But his heart is elsewhere. "After basketball is over, I'll spend more time with the kids," he promises. He'll be teaching Stockton family values to his children Houston, Michael, David and Lindsay. These are the values of gratitude and respect, even if, in life, there's no standing ovation at the end.

FEBRUARY 1, 1995
9,922 ASSISTS:
AMAZING RECORD!

"The Admiral"

"In basketball, the only credit I take is for using the gifts that God has given me. It's not my doing. In a way, it's not even me." David Robinson is a humble man, sometimes too humble. Sensitive, intelligent, and educated, he might have become a saxophonist, a jazz pianist, or a mathematician. Instead, he's a professional basketball player for the San Antonio Spurs and one of the best centers in the world. He's a refined man, 7'1" and 250 pounds, seemingly out of place in the world of professional sports.

David Maurice Robinson, unlike most, had never dreamed of becoming an NBA star. He preferred baseball as a kid. He was a good hitter and pitcher, and he was fast. At nine years old, he was already one of the best in his league. Robinson grew up in a picture-perfect part of Virginia, in a sheltered environment, pampered by his mother Freda and father Ambrose, who was a sonar operator in the U.S. Navy. It was an ideal world, starkly different from inner-city neighborhoods in the Bronx and Harlem where rising NBA hopefuls were battling each other on the courts.

David's interests were eclectic. Not only did he like football, golf, and bowling, but he enjoyed studying the piano, computers, and math. Sometimes he worked for hours, analyzing various theories and equations. He's an intellectual who still maintains that he was never interested in and never enjoyed basketball.

Robinson did not join his high school basketball team until his senior year. When he moved from Virginia Beach to Osbourn Park, the basketball coach, charmed

DAVID ROBINSON/THE ADMIRAL
Born on August 6, 1965 in Key West, Florida/7'1" 250 lbs/High School: Osbourn Park High School, Manassas, Virginia/College: The United States Naval Academy/Drafted by the San Antonio Spurs in 1987 in the first round (first overall pick)/Rookie of the Year in 1990/Leader in rebounds in 1991/Defensive Player of the Year in 1992/Leader in blocked shots in 1992/League leader in points scored in 1994/League MVP in 1995/All-NBA First Team in 1991, 1992, 1995 and 1996/All-Defensive First Team in 1991, 1992, 1995, and 1996/Seven All-Star Game appearances/1986 World Champion as member of the United States Team/Bronze medal in the 1988 Olympic Games/Member of Dream Teams I and III

by the 6'6" seventeen-year-old, asked Robinson to try-out—just for fun. It was an amazing show. Robinson immediately joined the starting five—but not with great enthusiasm. Again, he was only really interested in baseball, music, and math. After high school, he decided to enroll in the Navy—like his dad. It had been ages since the Navy had seen action in the Pacific, not to mention on the basketball court. The Midshipmen hadn't captured an NCAA title since 1960. But David Robinson couldn't care less. That's not why he was there. In fact, he was barely accepted into the Navy at all because the maximum height allowed was 6'7".

His first year was mediocre at best. David Robinson spent most of the games on the bench, a towel over his legs, getting barely seven points and four rebounds per game. But he was growing at a rate of two inches every year, and he managed to keep up his speed. During his second year, people started predicting a career in the NBA even though his life was not centered around basketball. For Robinson, basketball was only a game. His teammates, who dreamed of a life in the NBA, were speechless at his talent and irate at his nonchalance.

At the end of his second year Robinson sailed the Midshipmen to the NCAA tournament, a road not traveled for twenty-five years. The team was eliminated in the second round, but made it to the quarterfinals against Duke the following season. Robinson finished the season with 22.7 points, 13 rebounds, and 5.9 blocks per game. He led the country in rebounds and blocked shots.

In 1986, he decided to finish school, which meant serving at sea for at least five years after college. He expected to graduate the following year. Because Robinson had chosen a career in the Navy, he bid farewell to thoughts of the NBA. Today he looks back at his Navy years as a period of growth, as a lesson in patience and perseverance.

In the summer of 1986, the Navy gave Robinson leave to play with the U.S. National team, and he became a world champion in Madrid. Everything started to happen quickly. In 1987, David Robinson was national college Player of the Year with an average of 28.2 points, 11.8 rebounds, and 4.5 blocks in thirty-two games. The Navy was eliminated by Michigan in the first round of the finals, but Robinson, with his 50 points, had proven himself. He was the first player in

NCAA history to record more than 2,500 points and grab more than 1,300 rebounds, with a 60 percent field goal record. Was Robinson really meant to become a naval officer?

The Navy was accommodating, giving him authorization to serve two years after college instead of five. Robinson had earned a degree in mathematics. In 1988, he was drafted in the first round by the San Antonio Spurs, who were taking a gamble on him. The Spurs offered Robinson twenty-six million dollars for ten years—eight if one counts his two years of military service.

During those two years, he participated in the Pan-American Games and the Olympics. Unfortunately, they both proved disappointing, producing embarrassing memories for the star. Since Robinson hadn't been playing much and was primarily working out, he wasn't moving well. He says that what he really lost was his timing.

LEFT IN THE DUST
Even though the Texan can fly over Malone and build up his records, he's still missing what's important: the NBA championship ring.

The San Antonio managers were a little nervous, but they were soon reassured. In his first NBA game on November 4, 1988, the Spurs beat the Lakers by 20 points, 106–88. Robinson saved 23 points and snagged 17 rebounds. At the end of the game, he admitted to having been in a fog at the Olympics, and was greatly relieved by his comeback.

From there, Robinson's accolades mounted: he was 1990 Rookie of the Year, leader in rebounds in 1991 (13 per game), and Defensive Player of the Year and first in blocks in 1992—the same year he became only the third player in NBA history to be in the top ten in five categories. He was eighth in points (23.2 per game), fourth in rebounds (12.2), first in blocks (4.4), fifth in steals (2.3), and sixth in field goal percentage (55.1 percent). Robinson was chosen to play on the

THE ADMIRALS' TROPHIES

In 1994, David Robinson is the first center to be first in points scored since Bob McAdoo in 1976. In 1995, he was named player of the year.

Dream Team, but the main prize was still missing: the NBA title. Was it really that important to him?

In 1993, the Texas management brought in the unruly Dennis Rodman to help Robinson and the Spurs search for the Holy Grail. It was like putting together oil and water. They didn't understand each other in the least. Despite a good regular season, San Antonio was eliminated in the first round of the playoffs by the Utah Jazz. Robinson's accomplishments were again only individual: he finished as leader in points (29.8) after a legendary quadruple-double against Detroit (34 points, 10 rebounds, 10 blocked shots, and 10 assists), and he had an unbelievable final game against the Clippers. Robinson was battling with O'Neal to be scoring leader, and on the day of the final he hit 71 points! Up until that point, only four people in the NBA had totaled more than 70 in a game. Not even Jordan has accomplished this. The whole team backed up Robinson that day against the Clippers. Rodman, the day's second highest scorer, only had 8 points.

Robinson was the first center to lead the league in scoring since McAdoo in 1976, but he was nevertheless dissatisfied with the season's outcome. San Antonio lost against Houston in the Conference Finals. The next two years were disconcerting. In 1996, suffering from backache then from a fractured bone in the foot, David Robinson had a bad year and played only six games all in all. The "Admiral" was on the rocks. San Antonio claimed a disappointing 20 wins and 62 losses.

Rodman blurted out that Robinson's MVP title was a joke, saying he wasn't really a leader. He criticized Robinson for shining only in the regular season, "when the games don't matter." Perhaps Robinson is too shy and easy-going to lead a championship team. He admits to thinking about his kids during the games and losing his concentration. But Robinson feels great when people praise him for being successful in both his career and his private life. In the April '96 *Sports Illustrated*, Robinson questioned, "At what point do you stop running after money and glory? It's a rat race. It never ends." David Robinson is an honest man, and his faith keeps him going. He wants his life to have meaning; he doesn't want to float from one thing to the next. Yet he has succeeded in doing just that, which is perhaps his greatest victory. He is a quiet hero.

ROBINSON IS SENSITIVE, EDUCATED, AND INTELLIGENT. HE FEELS FREEST PLAYING HIS SAX

Isiah Thomas

On September 21, 1991, when NBC revealed the names of the stars chosen for the first Dream Team, a major player seemed to be missing: Isiah Thomas, the explosive guard for the Pistons. Was it on purpose? The local press lashed out. Isiah Thomas calmly explained that he disturbs people. After all, he played with the most disrespected team in the league, he was the president of the Players' Association, and he didn't get along with Michael Jordan. Perhaps now he was paying the price. A furious Jack McCloskey, the Pistons' general manager, stormed out on the Olympic committee. He too suspected that the selectors were making the Bad Boys pay for their reputations. Detroit simmered. Only coach Chuck Daly went along with the selection crew. Isiah Thomas was bitter. He wanted to play with the team, but he was misunderstood—an outcast. Only the fans seemed to appreciate this gifted athlete with a big mouth. As a result, Isiah Thomas has snapped up every award imaginable, except for an Olympic gold.

Everyone has heard his story. One day when his teammate Bill Laimbeer was talking about eating lobster and caviar as a kid, Isiah Thomas burst out that Bill was lucky, because he had been forced to hunt rats to survive. Thomas was born on April 30, 1961, on West Madison Street, in the toughest and poorest neighborhood of Chicago. Isiah was the youngest of nine children. His mother, Maria, was a proud woman whose dignity was her ultimate refuge. The family often had nothing to eat, and she sometimes had to beg to be able to feed her children. As she claims, "It makes you hard, it teaches you about life." Mary Thomas overprotected her baby boy, fearing that he might take a wrong turn like

ISIAH THOMAS
Born on April 30, 1961 in Chicago, Illinois/6'1" 180 lbs/High School: St. Joseph High School, Chicago/College: Indiana/NCAA champion in 1981/Most Outstanding Player of the NCAA tournament, 1981/Drafted by the Detroit Pistons (second overall pick)/Wins NBA title in 1989 and 1990 with the Detroit Pistons/Leader in assists in 1985/Finals MVP in 1990/All-NBA First Team in 1984, 1985 and 1986/Twelve All-Star Game appearances; MVP in 1984 and 1986

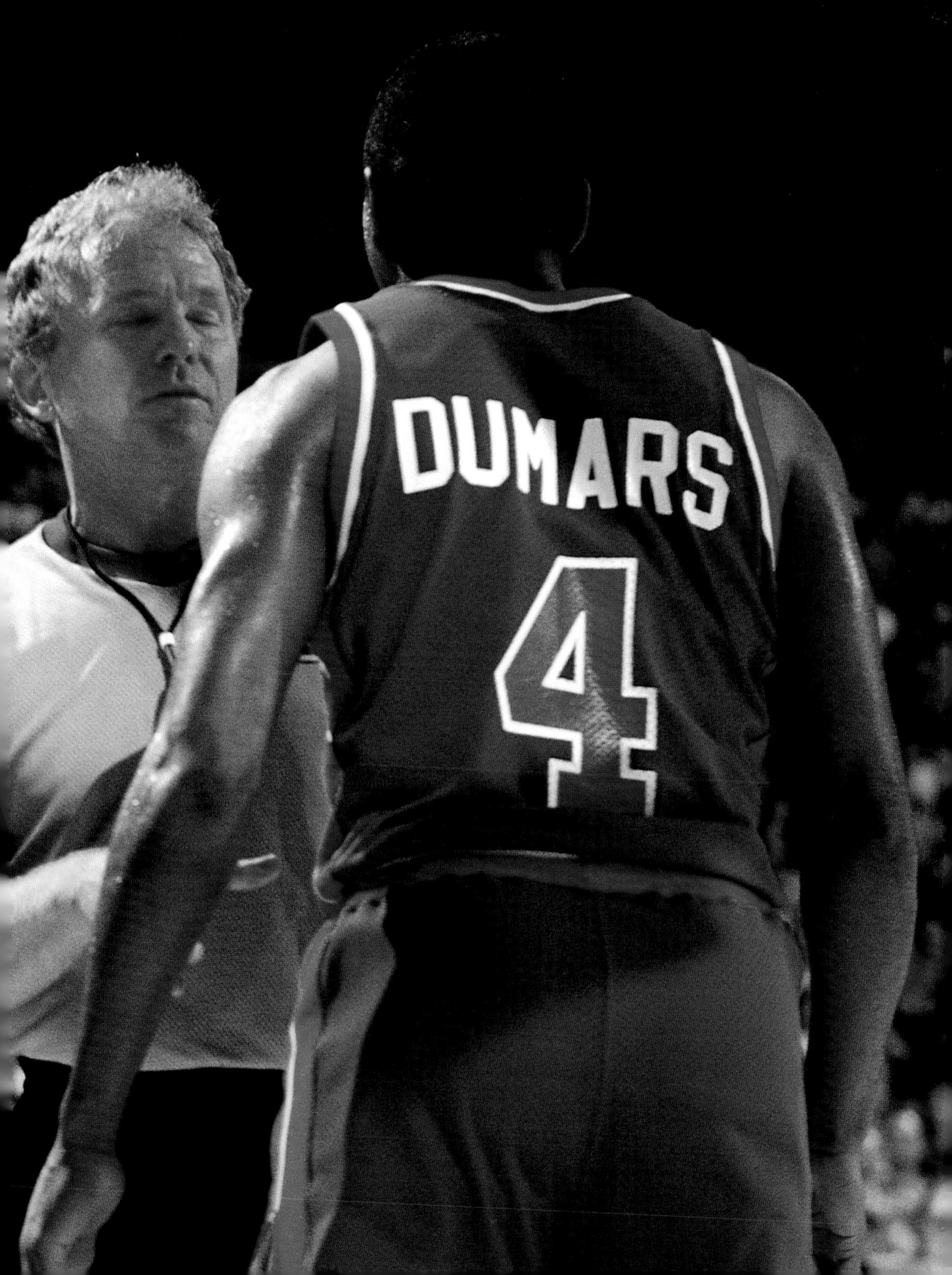
DUMARS
4

three of his older brothers who fell to drugs and delinquency. She got help from a man named Gene Pintagore.

Pintagore was the coach at St. Joseph High School, a mostly white Catholic school on the other side of town. He spotted Isiah during a game and asked him if he would be interested in joining his school's team. Hoping to provide a good future for her son, Mary Thomas encouraged him to join, and his life took off in a new direction. Isiah quickly received a scholarship and just as quickly became the leader of the team. Pintagore kept a close eye on him, and as a result, it only took three months for St. Joseph to develop the best high school team in Illinois, with a record of 73 wins and 15 losses. Isiah's stats were extraordinary: 24 points, 7 assists, 6 rebounds, and 5 steals per game. The school had never had such an all-around player.

Colleges were fighting for Thomas. Mark Aguirre, his pal from the playground (who would be first draft pick in 1981), suggested that he go with him to nearby De Paul, but Gene Pintagore encouraged him towards Indiana—and that's where Thomas ended up. The year was 1979, and Isiah Thomas, the kid from Chicago, took off for the middle of nowhere in Indiana. He would set the place on fire. The coach, Bobby Knight, had a reputation for being a hard-liner—and that's putting it nicely. His rules were meant to be obeyed; players worked hard under his iron fist. It was like the Army, and there was no room for show-boats and clowns. As it turns out, however, Isiah was a showman—the sly guy who left you helpless when he dribbled through his legs, switched hands, and passed behind your back for a lay-up. Although the fans loved Thomas' tricks, Knight was less approving. Their relationship quickly soured, but the season's results overshadowed their differences: in 1980, the Hoosiers lost to Purdue in the regional finals (76–69), but in 1981, they beat North Carolina to become NCAA champions (63–50). Isiah Thomas scored 23 points and was elected Most Valuable Player. He also led Indiana in points scored, assists, and steals for two seasons. Still, Thomas was missing one title—Olympic champion—and he didn't have the chance to capture it in 1980, when the United States decided to boycott the Games in Moscow. Isiah had been chosen for the team—but fate had other plans.

In 1981, Thomas was the second overall draft pick. He was off to Detroit, and the Pistons became the Bad Boys. Although he already had a reputation as a trash-talker, he didn't think it was out of arrogance. He protested that he was only 6'1", and had to defend himself if he wanted to survive in the NBA. With Thomas as their leader, the Pistons finally got things rolling. Chuck Daly gave the team full credit for their success. All he did, he said, was hop along for the ride. The figures spoke for themselves. During 13 years in the NBA, Isiah was elected to play in the All-Star Game 12 times and was named All-Star MVP twice; he was named three times to the All-NBA First Team; he was leader in assists in 1985, won the championship in 1989 and 1990, and was the 1990 Finals MVP. Aside from Larry Bird, Magic Johnson, and Michael Jordan, few players in the last 20 years could claim to have achieved so much.

Both Bird and Magic played key roles in Thomas' career. Magic is a real friend. The two call each other up, hang out, and would sometimes give each other a

SOME HOSTILITY (pp. 170–171)
Isiah Thomas' Pistons attack the referee during the fourth game of the finals in 1990.
Their nickname: The Bad Boys.
THE INHERITOR (below)
In 1996, Isiah Thomas hands over the Rookie of the Year trophy to Damon Stoudamire.

hug before their teams went to battle. The fans savored their meetings. In the 1988 finals, Isiah Thomas brought the series to a seventh game by slamming home 25 points in one quarter—an NBA record. The Lakers won it in the end by three points (108–105) in the epic seventh game. Magic once let slip that in order to beat the Pistons, you had to know how to hate them.

Thomas' relationship with Jordan, on the other hand, was much colder. For years, Detroit prevented Chicago from getting past the Conference Final. In 1990, Isiah single-handedly eliminated the Bulls with 29 points, 11 assists, and 8 rebounds in the last game of the Conference Finals. But, when Jordan heard that Thomas wouldn't be going to Barcelona, he merely remarked that he wasn't the one who chose the Olympic team.

Isiah Thomas had countless legendary games, but one of the most famous was against Denver in December 1983. On that day, he beat a personal record by scoring 47 points. The final score: 186–184 after three overtimes, which wore out the Pistons completely. Unfortunately, on April 19, 1994, Isiah Thomas tore his achilles tendon during a game with Orlando and ended his career prematurely. He was only thirty-three, and had just been chosen to play for the World Championships in Toronto with Dream Team II. It was a stroke of bad luck…

But Thomas is a smart man. A few months later, he traded in his uniform for a three-piece suit and took charge of recruiting for the new Toronto franchise. He felt at home. In his first draft, he chose Damon Stoudamire from the University of Arizona as seventh pick. Many were surprised, but Thomas was thrilled. Stoudamire is his clone; he has the same speed and agility, and the same foresight as Thomas. He's even a showman. The Toronto guard finished fifth in assists for the year and was nominated 1996 Rookie of the Year. The fans love him. Everyone is already talking about Stoudamire leading the Dream Team IV or V, perhaps even in the Sydney Games. Isiah has the ticket to his revenge.

"The Beast"

E

Patrick Ewing

You've probably seen it. After every game, Patrick Ewing carefully and methodically puts a giant ice pack on each knee, because his joints have gotten old too soon. Ewing is a worn-out player—drained, tired of running for more than ten years after an NBA title that he'll most probably never own, tired of carrying the hopes of an old New York franchise on his shoulders. The Knicks haven't won the title since 1973.

Patrick Ewing was twelve when he and his family came to the United States from Kingston, Jamaica, a country where basketball was little known. He had never taken an interest in it, he didn't even know the rules. The newcomers landed right across from Boston, just like the pilgrims. It was a difficult time. Dorothy and Carl Ewing worked hard to feed their children, and Patrick didn't much like school, where the court was king. But one day, because of his size (6'1" at thirteen-years-old), his classmates asked, "Hey, do you wanna play basketball?" Ewing was soon crushing his opponents, and the school's records were quickly re-written. They became state champions three times.

Never mind the report cards, what was increasingly important were his stat sheets. Ewing was a true talent. Coach John Thompson of Georgetown was notified and headed out to the school. Six months later, Patrick Ewing packed his bags for the NCAA's top-rate Georgetown University. Thompson had a reputation for his defensive tactics, usually built around one of the best centers in the country. Ewing, Mourning, and Mutombo all graduated from Georgetown.

At Georgetown Thompson was not only Ewing's coach but also his spiritual

PATRICK EWING/THE BEAST
Born on August 5, 1962 in Kingston, Jamaica/7'0" 240 lbs/High School: Rindge and Latin, Cambridge, Massachusetts/College: Georgetown University/NCAA champion in 1984/Most Outstanding Player of the NCAA tournament in 1984/Rookie of the Year in 1986/Selected to the All-NBA First Team in 1990/Ten All-Star Game appearances/Gold medal in the 1984 Olympic Games/Member of Dream Team I

father. In his first year, 1982, Ewing led Georgetown to the finals against Michael Jordan. But North Carolina defeated Georgetown by one point (63–62). Nevertheless, Georgetown achieved the title two years later in 1984 against Houston: 84–75.

The summer of that same year, Patrick Ewing went to the Olympics for the first time. The super-strict coach, Bobby Knight, wanted him for the Los Angeles Games. The Games were a triumph. With Jordan, Mullin, Perkins, Tisdale, and Ewing, the United States presented the best team ever seen at the Games (until 1992). Jordan was elected MVP, but Ewing, a real giver, finished third in points, and second in rebounds. In all, he averaged 11 points and 5.6 rebounds per game. In 1985, Georgetown lost again in the finals, this time against Villanova (66–64). But that same year, Ewing received the *Sporting News* College Player of the Year Award. He also became one of the best defensive players in college basketball history, leaving Georgetown with an average of 15.3 points, 9.2 rebounds, and 3.4 blocks in 143 games. It was time to climb the ranks of the NBA.

Every team wanted Ewing—so did the reporters. But Ewing was not very talkative by nature unlike Charles Barkley who had a huge appetite for a good interview. Ewing says he doesn't want to stir up any controversies, and will let his playing do the talking. The NBA initiated its draft lottery in 1985, and the New York Knicks had the first overall pick. The managers rejoiced and of course selected Ewing. The Big Apple, a hungry, volatile, and demanding city, awaited him.

Madison Square Garden, the Knicks' inner sanctum, is located in the heart of Manhattan. This legendary stadium has been home to the greatest athletes of all time, from the worlds of basketball, boxing, hockey, and tennis. It's where New York comes to scream and holler for the whole world to hear. Spike Lee, Madonna, Cindy Crawford, John McEnroe, Woody Allen, and Michael Douglas all come to cheer on the Knicks. It is Hollywood on the Hudson, and in no other city is pressure from the press more intense.

Unfortunately, what happened on the court after Ewing's arrival wasn't quite as interesting as who was in the stands. The Knicks couldn't win a thing. Ewing scored an average 20 points per game every year (he peaked with 28.6 points in

1989–90). With five coaches in five years, New York reached the semifinals twice, in 1989 and 1990. It was disastrous. Ewing was far from happy, and he was also starting to worry.

In the summer of 1991, Pat Riley came to New York. Riley led the Lakers to seven finals, winning the title four times. He was the coach of the eighties. With his Armani suits, slicked-back hair, and tough-as-leather attitude, he declared that it was time to concentrate on the team. The days of individual stardom were over. Riley's strategy worked out well for the Knicks, because Ewing, Oakley, Mason, Smith, and Starks had what it took to play a tough game.

New York went to the Conference Semifinals in 1992 (the year in which Ewing

SIMPLY THE "BEAST" (p. 183)
The dunk is still one of his favorite weapons.
NEW YORK–CHICAGO (below)
Ewing against Longley. One of the must-see power battles of the nineties.
Unfortunately, Ewing rarely comes out the winner.

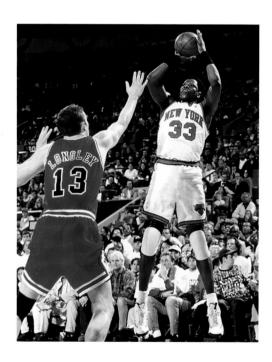

was also an Olympic gold medalist for the second time), reached the Conference Finals in 1993, and the NBA finals in 1994. At last. Chicago and Michael Jordan weren't there to stop them in the Eastern Conference. Ewing knew it was now or never. At age thirty-two, he didn't have much more time to capture the Big One. The only thing standing in his way was the Houston Rockets.

In 1994, the finals swung back and forth. Everything that could happen did. It was Ewing against Olajuwon, a duel of giants. Fouls showered down, and before the final seventh game a *Houston Post* columnist wrote, "Oh grace, come back to this game in which the players would run like gazelles, were as graceful as ballet dancers, and had the flight time of *Apollo* astronauts." Ewing ignored the commentary. For him, as for many New Yorkers, the title was the only thing that counted. Stats weren't important. What mattered was the ring. "If I don't win this title, it will be a huge let-down."

New York, leading three games to two in the finals, lost in the end, four games to three (90–84 in the last game). The fairy tale came to an end. In the spring of 1995, Riley resigned and was replaced by Don Nelson, who was himself replaced by one of his assistants, Jeff Van Gundy, in the middle of the year. The results were no better.

Ewing, one of the best centers of all time, had to his credit one college title, two Olympic gold medals, two shot knees, and an ache that ice packs could never relieve.

Patrick Ewing was giving his all. He'd never captured the title with the Knicks in more than ten years on the team. He didn't care about stats. The only thing that mattered was the ring. New York had been chasing after the title since 1973.

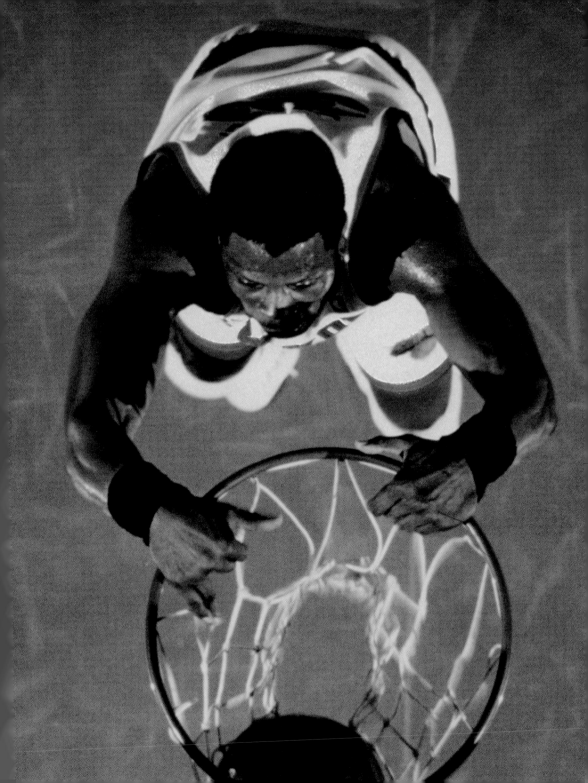

Clyde Drexler

"The Glide"

There is only one thing that hasn't gone right for Clyde Drexler—he's a contemporary of Michael Jordan's, and plays the same position. If he weren't, he might be the most talented and acclaimed player of his generation. He might be a star. Drexler is a simple, lovable, and generous man who has spent his career far from the drama of Hollywood and Broadway, far from the star system. For twelve years he has played in Portland, a city with a human face, removed from intense media attention. He enjoys being away from the buzz, living with his wife and children in peace. No matter what Drexler's view on stardom is, he's one of the most outstanding players of the past 20 years. He's the stuff of which heroes are made.

As a child, Drexler was a big fan of his hometown teams in Houston, the Rockets and the Astros. Though he was born in New Orleans, his family moved to Texas where the young Clyde immediately headed for the playgrounds. There was one court in the middle of town frequented by all the best players in the area. Sometimes he even got some time with pro players and college stars. As a teen, he met Moses Malone, who befriended him and taught him a lot—as did Robert Reid. Clyde listened. At the time, it was all just for fun. But when he reached his senior year in high school, he took things more seriously. He wanted a career and a scholarship.

Clyde wasn't a star, but his friend Michael Young (Drexler said he was the best young player in Texas, and he went on to become European champion with Limoges in 1993) was. Young was wooed by the University of Houston Cougars, and when he accepted, he had Drexler at his side. "This guy is good," he told the managers. His plan worked. Without Young, Drexler says, he might not be where he is today.

CLYDE DREXLER/THE GLIDE
Born on June 22, 1962 in New Orleans, Louisiana/6'7" 222 lbs/High School: Sterling High School, Texas/College: University of Houston/Drafted by the Portland Trail Blazers in 1983 (fourteenth overall pick)/NBA title with the Houston Rockets in 1995/All-NBA First Team in 1992/Nine All-Star Game appearances/Member of Dream Team I

It was a golden age in basketball. The year was 1981, and while Phi Slamma Jamma did not exactly revolutionize college basketball, they certainly added excitement to a conventional game. The following year, Drexler, Olajuwon, and Young charged to the Final Four but lost in the semifinal against North Carolina and Jordan. A year later, the fraternity reached the finals after a bold and historic semifinal against Louisville. It was the peak of Drexler's college career. In the finals, however, Houston fell to North Carolina State when Lorenzo Charles sank a basket in the last second. Nevertheless, despite his short college career, Drexler was the first Cougar to score more than 1,000 points, snatch more than 900 rebounds, and dish out more than 300 assists.

Drexler decided to skip his senior year and head for the NBA. The so-so high school player had become "The Glide," on account of his prowess in leaping from the free throw line to slam dunk fifteen feet away. What a flight. Drexler is a gymnast and a dancer, elegant, graceful, and fast. He can go coast-to-coast, and

perform all kinds of offensive wizardry. He could easily have been nicknamed Clyde "Air" Drexler.

Drexler's story picks up again in Portland where he was selected by the Trail Blazers as the fourteenth overall pick in the 1983 draft, way behind Sampson, Stipanovitch, McCray, Scott, and many others. But the Blazers had foresight.

The first few years were difficult, because Drexler, like many artists, worked by himself. Several of the Oregon head coaches couldn't stand the individualism (they referred to his "tantrums"). Jack Ramsay and Mike Schuler didn't last on the team, but Drexler did. Drexler found support

from coach Rick Adelman, who avoided any tactics that constricted Drexler's style. Adelman's approach proved to be effective. In 1990, the Blazers reached the NBA finals but went down to the Pistons four games to one. In 1991, the Los Angeles Lakers defeated them in the Conference Finals, four games to two. Some people called them losers but *The Sporting News* favored them to win the upcoming 1992 title. Portland proved themselves in the regular season, and reached the finals for the second time in three years. But, the hardest hurdle still remained. They had to beat the Bulls.

Magic Johnson grinned. He knew Michael Jordan likes the kind of game where he can show who's best. In the finals, Jordan strung together 35 points in the first half. The message was clear. Jordan (MVP of the season and the finals) was the greatest player of his generation, perhaps of all time. The Blazers took a beating, losing four games to two. Drexler was consoled by his gold medal summer with the Dream Team in Barcelona. Christian Laettner and Drexler were the last two accepted onto the team. The Glide secured his place at the last minute, a little like the coming title with Houston.

In February 1995, both the Rockets and

the Blazers were sluggish. Drexler knew Portland had missed its chance to become the champions, and Houston, who finished sixth in the Western Conference, knew they could use a boost from Drexler to get out of their rut. In mid-February, Drexler and Tracy Murray were traded for Otis Thorpe. Although Drexler was greatly respected, many thought that Tomjanovich and the Houston management had made a mistake. It was true that Olajuwon and Drexler were friends. It was true they were from Phi Slamma Jamma. But the Blazers guard was already thirty-three years old. What could he bring to a team that was so used to Thorpe? Drexler fit right into the Houston line-up, immediately offering the Rockets quickness and skill. Even if Houston had lost one of their scorers, and Olajuwon was more alone up front, they could make up for their loss in speed. Teammate Robert Horry says Drexler drove him crazy because he was years older, and yet ran faster, as if he were a kid. "But he does get you up off your butt."

Houston's journey through the playoffs was exciting. They swept the finals against Orlando and the rising Magic superstars. For Drexler, it was the title that would keep him playing. Olajuwon added, "This title, I only wanted it for him."

Drexler isn't Jordan, but it doesn't matter. Nobody's perfect. Drexler knows you just have to try to be yourself. Every summer he gives a little bit back, trying to get kids interested in basketball, and warning them about drugs through his summer camps. He has a message: Drexler isn't the world's best player—he's better. He's an example for others—and a role model for kids.

THE GLIDE (previous page)
One day Drexler flew up 11'1'' to dunk.
BIRD'S-EYE VIEW (right)
The Houston-Orlando game in the 1995–1996 season. Replay of the previous year's final.

IN 1995, DREXLER JOINS HIS BUDDY OLAJUWON TO TAKE HOME THE ILLUSTRIOUS NBA TITLE.

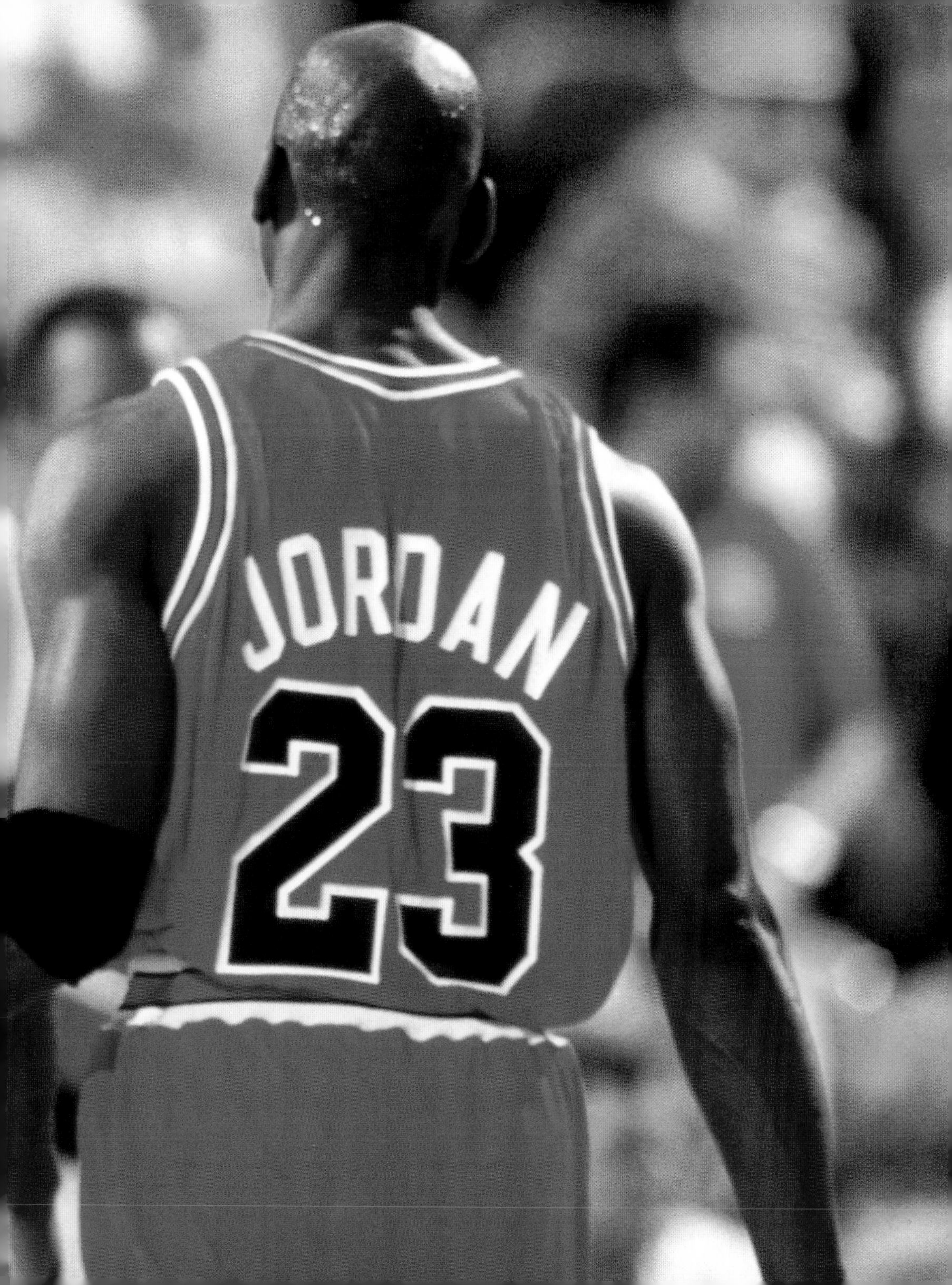
JORDAN
23

Grant Hill

Grant Hill is America's sweetheart. He's good-looking, polite, and courteous, humble and intelligent. He's also a multidimensional star who has received the highest praise, in fact, too much for his own taste. In February 1995, when 1,289,585 Americans voted for him to start in the All-Star Game in Phoenix, he apologized profusely to the other players. It was the first time in NBA history that a rookie had gotten the most votes for an All-Star Game, but he wanted to stay out of the spotlight. It was the same story in 1996 when the public dared to prefer him to Michael Jordan, who was back on the court. Hill was flattered, but thought everyone was nuts; he was only twenty-three years old and hadn't proven anything yet. Unlike most rising stars, he steered clear of the limelight.

Hill was lucky to have grown up under a roof where strong principles and politeness were the rule. But he would always have to prove himself more than others. It is not easy to forge ahead when one's legitimacy is based on the overwhelming glory of a rich and famous father. Grant Hill is the son of former Dallas Cowboys running back Calvin Hill. Still, Grant Hill likes to lay low. What pushes him is the desire to show that his success has nothing to do with what he inherited, but with what he can do.

Grant Hill was born on October 5, 1972, in Dallas. He is a child of the jet-set. After Calvin Hill and the Cowboys won the Super Bowl, the country was buzzing about the triumphs of this exquisite athlete, who was now also a rich man. Grant's mother Janet was the head of a legal and financial consulting firm, and amongst her close friends was her college roommate, Hillary Clinton. The Hill family was wealthy, and they didn't hide it, buying antiques, collecting fancy cars, traveling, and attending all sorts of social events. They lived the American

GRANT HILL
Born on October 5, 1972 in Dallas, Texas/6'8'' 225 lbs/High School: South Lakes High School, Reston, Virginia/College: Duke University/NCAA Champion in 1991 and 1992/Drafted by the Detroit Pistons in 1994 (third overall pick)/Rookie of the Year in 1995/All-NBA First Team in 1997/Three All-Star Game appearances/Member of the Dream Team III

dream. Grant's young friends constantly asked him questions about his father, and envied him for being able to go into a Washington Redskins' (Calvin's new team) locker room after a game. Six-year-old Grant withdrew. He didn't want to be seen as a rich kid, and especially hated it when his father pulled up to his school in a Porsche while the other kids looked on. One day, he was introduced to the U.S ambassador in London, the next, he met Senator Bill Bradley. Then there was a family lunch with the president of Harvard. His was a golden childhood.

When it came to sports, Grant wanted to play football at first, like his dad. But his father resisted the idea, fearing that hasty comparisons between himself and his son would upset his development. Grant's father was always there to help him make the right choices in all kinds of areas. So instead, Grant gave soccer a whirl, and then at age ten, he tried basketball. He was great at it. Calvin followed his progress and gave him advice, but was also very strict with him. After every game, Grant even got a personal debriefing; whatever he did, it was never good enough. One afternoon when he was thirteen years old, his father challenged him to a one-on-one game, hoping to teach young Grant a few things. Of course, it was the other way round.

Grant was at the top of his class in all subjects in school, including sports. He was a three-time North Virginia Player of the Year as a member of the South Lakes High School team and won the championship his junior year. By the time he was a senior, all the colleges had their eyes on the boy with an average of 25 points, 11 rebounds, and 8 assists. His father was pushing for North Carolina, his mother Georgetown, but Hill wanted to go to Duke for its academic tradition.

There he blossomed. Duke coach Mike Krzyzewski called him the best player he had ever had

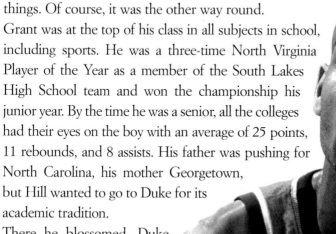

under his command. But the competition was tough. When Grant Hill joined the Blue Devils in 1990, the team had just lost to UNLV in the NCAA finals—but Laettner and Hurley promised a better future for the team. Hill watched and soaked up everything. With a season average of 11.2 points and 5.1 rebounds, he went on to help win the title in 1991 against Kansas. The next year Duke repeated. They became college champions by beating Michigan by twenty points in the finals, as Hill captivated the crowd with 18 points, 10 rebounds, and 5 assists. He was clearly a leader. Calvin applauded him. In 1993, with Laettner gone, Hill was the one to become the star—not Hurley. Unfortunately, he injured himself towards the end of the season, and wasn't up to par for the final tournament. The Blue Devils were eliminated in the second round—but they would recover the following year. In 1994, they went to the finals for the third time in four years, a triumph in itself, but Duke fell in the final seconds to

HILL MOVES A MOUNTAIN (p. 206)
At 24, Grant Hill has already twice been the most voted player to start in the All-Star Game and has an Olympic gold medal won with the Dream Team III.
MY FATHER THE HERO (below)
Calvin Hill, ex-football player, watches over his son's career and reckons he has always had things easy.

Arkansas, Bill Clinton's team. The president was in the stands to witness the victory of his alma mater.

Two months after the loss against Arkansas, one of Hill's first calls was from the White House, congratulating him for being the Piston's third overall pick in the draft. Grant didn't want to boast, but it was exactly where he wanted to go. He really didn't care about the sixty-eight million dollars picked up by the arrogant Glenn Robinson, Milwaukee's number one pick. Hill signed with Detroit for forty-five million, and hurried to get himself ready for the upcoming season. Detroit needed Grant Hill. The former Bad Boys, the 1989 and 1990 champions, had just ended a catastrophic year and wanted a new start with Hill. Many journalists saw a new Michael Jordan in him—the same first step, the same takeoff, the same grace. Hill is modest, though, and America was seduced by his charm.

He is more of a giver than Jordan. Don Cheney, his old coach said he did what the team needed, and Mike Krzyzewski noted that there wasn't an aspect of the game he hadn't totally mastered. In his first year, Grant Hill got an average of 19.9 points, 6.4 rebounds, and 5 assists per game. He had Jordan's elegance and Pippen's stats. He was an incredibly complete player. The following year, his numbers got even better: 20.2 points, 8.1 rebounds, and 6 assists. And his third year was better still: 21.4 points, 9 rebounds and 7.3 assists per game. The Pistons had been oiled. There were no more bumps and grinds; with Hill playing for them, Detroit went from 20 to 28 wins in the first year, from 28 to 46 in the second year, and from 46 to 54 in the third. On top of all this came a first selection in the All-NBA First Team in 1997. "I don't show it," said Hill, "but when I'm on the court, I consider myself to be the best player of all, and no one can stop me."

If Detroit is one day champion again, it will without a doubt be because of Grant Hill. The golden child has become a golden man. His old teammate Oliver Miller predicts that soon kids won't say they want to play like Jordan, they will want to play like Hill. For the moment, however, Grant, a grateful son, offered his Rookie of the Year award (shared with Jason Kidd) to Calvin, who rushed to find a place for it among his own trophies. Janet, a bit mischievously, calls it the ego room. Later on, Hill secretly hopes to go into politics. And what luck, because his mother just happens to know someone who could give him a hand.

Anfernee Hardaway
"Penny"

It's the end of May 1993 and the Orlando Magic have won the NBA draft lottery for the second year in a row. They had a one in sixty-six chance, but their ticket was pulled out first. They hit the jackpot. A couple of weeks later, on June 30, the Magic headed out to Detroit where the draft had taken place to make Chris Webber an official team member. At least, that's what everybody thought. The fans were as excited as the management about the forward from Michigan, and all the papers knew about the deal. Who wouldn't dream of bringing the best college player of the season together with Shaquille O'Neal, the best college player of the previous one? There was no doubt. The ceremony was broadcast throughout the country, and close to ten thousand people had bought tickets to celebrate in the Orlando arena. Everything was set—the giant screen, the popcorn, the hot dogs. Now they just had to wait.

This was the set-up for one of the biggest surprises in the history of the draft. Even though Chris Webber was Orlando's first pick, he was traded less than an hour later to the Golden State Warriors for Hardaway, who had been selected third. Orlando fans were furious, especially with general manager Pat Williams. Within a few weeks, however, they would thank Williams for having dared to make such a decision. Magic Johnson said that watching Hardaway play was like looking in the mirror. Could there possibly be a better compliment?

Anfernee Hardaway's story could have just as easily taken a different turn. He was born Anfernee Deon Hardaway on July 18, 1972, in Elvis' own Memphis, Tennessee. His neighborhood was plagued by drugs and crime. It was the landscape for Jailhouse Rock, the background for a classic tale of sorrow. Anfernee saw his father for the first time when he was six-years-old, when his

ANFERNEE HARDAWAY/PENNY HARDAWAY
Born on July 18, 1972 in Memphis, Tennessee/6'7" 200 lbs/High School: Treadwell High School, Memphis/College: Memphis State/Drafted by the Golden State Warriors in 1993 (third overall pick)/Named to the All-NBA First Team in 1995 and 1996/Three All-Star Game appearances/Member of the Dream Team III

212

mother left home to try to make it as a singer in a nightclub in California. His grandmother, Louise, was his only family. She took him under her wing, bringing him to her home where nine cousins all lived together in the same room. She made him work hard so that he could "be somebody" one day. He was lucky. She woke him up at six o'clock every morning and then walked him directly to the school doors. She worked in the cafeteria. At night, she oversaw his homework and on Sunday took him to the Early Grove Baptist Church. One day, Louise gave him the nickname that he would keep for the rest of his life, "Pretty," which eventually evolved into "Penny."

Penny often says he has two loves in his life—his grandmother and basketball. By the time he was nine-years-old, he was already an ace at the sport, constantly challenging the older kids to a game. As a child, his idol was Magic Johnson, whom he watched on TV whenever he could. Johnson was a hero at Treadwell High School, in Memphis, a school that came within an inch of capturing the state championship title. In high school, Hardaway's statistics were impressive: the young star got more than 36 points, more than 10 rebounds, and more than 6 assists on average in his senior year. In the meantime, his mother returned and wanted her son back. Hardaway's family turmoil led to problems in school, and in the second semester of his senior year he was declared "academically ineligible" to participate in the MacDonald's All-American Game, the All-Star Game for high school students.

Getting into college was a big hurdle for Hardaway. In fact, it took some help from Memphis State coach Larry Finch. Hardaway's grandmother Louise, as always, took care of everything else, surveying the situation, and straightening out the young man, who could think of nothing but basketball. She told him that basketball wasn't the passport to a successful adult life, and Penny listened. He started to work hard. She was strict with him, but Hardaway would eventually agree that respectability wasn't attained only by building up stats.

On April 28, 1991, at 20 years of age, Anfernee Hardaway came face-to-face with life-threatening danger. He and a friend went out to visit his cousin LeMarcus Golden. The boys parked, stepped out of their car, and had just slammed the door, when another sedan that had been cruising the area eased up behind them.

The window rolled down. There were four men inside. Anfernee barely had time to answer a trick question when he found himself alongside his friend, face-down on the pavement, a gun at his head. They broke out in a cold sweat as they both were victimized in an everyday hold-up. As the muggers pulled away, they fired some shots to protect their escape, and one ricocheted off of Penny's foot. Hardaway says he saw death in the face, and didn't understand why he hadn't been killed. "In a case like this, all you have time to think about is death, I was sure they were going to kill me." Understandably, it took him a while to get over it. In addition, the doctors were worried they might damage a nerve, so they waited until October to remove the bullet from his foot. Luckily, Hardaway

TYRA BANKS, MODEL (p. 213)
There's a little Tennessee in all of us...
BAD NEWS IN THE STARS (below)
O'Neal and Hardaway only dreamed about one thing: capturing the NBA title.
But Shaq left, leaving Penny alone to do the impossible.

would still be able to play. From that point on, Hardaway saw the world in another light, and the results could be seen both on and off the court.

Because of his academic problems, Hardaway wasn't eligible to play with the Memphis State Tigers in 1990–91, but he was able to pay the next year. He was untouchable: 17.4 points, 7 rebounds, and 5.5 assists his first year; and 22.8 points, 8.5 rebounds, and 6.4 assists his second year. He was an all-around player. Nolen Richardson, Arkansas' famous coach, maintained: "Take Magic Johnson and Michael Jordan, mix them together, and you get Anfernee Hardaway." In June 1992, Hardaway was called for a warm-up against the Dream Team with a group of kids who had little respect for legends. The game was only 20 minutes long, but the college gang inflicted the only loss the Dream Team ever suffered. Hardaway was the mirror image of Magic Johnson. Louise was proud, and the

GOING SOUTH FOR THE WINTER

On the day he drafts Hardaway, Orlando General Manager Pat Williams announces that he has found the player that will carry the franchise for the next fifteen years.

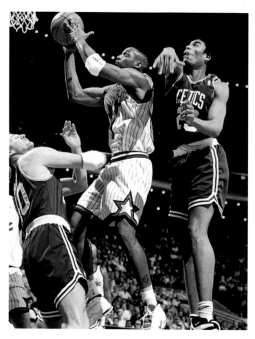

NBA was impressed. Realizing he didn't need to finish college in order to move up, Hardaway entered the 1993 draft. He knew Orlando was keen on Webber, but with the help of his agent Carl Poston, he put pressure on the Florida management to make the deal fall through. He succeeded in making them think twice by asking, "What are you going to do with another forward like Webber when what you need is a guard like me to feed balls to O'Neal?" Bob Huggins, the Cincinnati coach, drove the point home, declaring that any team that would pass up Hardaway was as stupid as the one that let Jordan go by in 1984. The night before the draft, the Magic management, feeling more and more uncertain about Webber, called Hardaway to a practice session with Scott, Turner, Bowie, and others at the Orlando arena. Orlando gave in. They now sought Hardaway. The Webber trade was finalized two hours before the draft.

In his first game in an Orlando uniform, against Philadelphia, Hardaway got into foul trouble. Pat Williams held his position that the Magic had found the player that would carry the franchise for the next fifteen years. Hardaway lived up to the prediction. On November 23, he scored 23 points, snatched 8 rebounds, and made 5 assists against Webber and the Golden State Warriors. He received a standing ovation. Hardaway finished the season averaging 16.9 points, 6.6 assists, and 5.4 rebounds. It is hard to be a more complete rookie. In fact, he was the only rookie to start in all 82 games of the regular season that year. What's more, Shaq and Hardaway complemented each other extremely well. Hardaway anticipates that one day the Magic will be crowned champions.

Even though many saw O'Neal and Hardaway as a nineties version of Johnson and Abdul-Jabbar, the two weren't able to capture the title. In 1994, the Magic were eliminated in the first round of the playoffs and were defeated by Houston in the finals the following year in a 4–0 sweep. Hardaway, despite his 20.9 points and 7.2 assists during the regular season, wasn't really "on" in the finals— perhaps he was a bit too young for the pressure. Nevertheless, journalists named him one of the top five players in 1995 and in 1996, the same year in which the Magic were swept by Chicago in the Conference Finals.

"I don't want to be one of the best basketball players in the world, I want to be the best as soon as Jordan is gone," Hardaway announced. He might well have

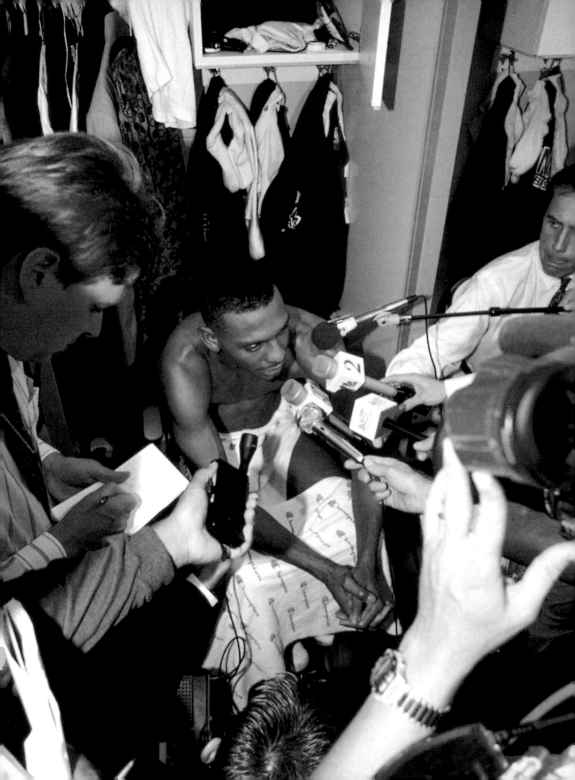

"I don't want to be one of the best, I want to be the best as soon as Jordan has gone," claims Penny. "Take Magic and Jordan, mix it all together and you get Hardaway," declared Arkansas coach Nolan Richardson.

a chance. Houston guru Rudy Tomjanovich calls him the new Magic Johnson.

Now that Shaq is no longer in Orlando, the team's management had to step in to fulfill Hardaway's ambitions. The negotiations were tough, but Hardaway signed on at a price of close to seventy million dollars for a little more than ten years. This gives him plenty of time to secure a championship ring. As for Louise, she no longer has to work in the school cafeteria and now lives in a beautiful red brick house in a fancy neighborhood of Memphis. Pat Williams, general manager of the Orlando Magic, is simply grateful: "Don't change a thing with the Lottery, it's the best system around."

M

Reggie Miller

June 1, 1994, was a sacred day for Indiana pro basketball. The Pacers met the Knicks for the fifth game of the Conference Finals at Madison Square Garden. The teams were tied at two games apiece, and New York was leading by twelve points in the final quarter, when Reggie Miller went into a trance and had an historic quarter. The baby-faced man unleashed five three-pointers in a row, and twenty-five points in twelve brief minutes—thirty-nine points in all. Teammate Byron Scott took him by the arm. "Don't touch me," cried Miller. He'd been touched by God. On the sidelines, Knicks fanatic Spike Lee howled. Miller pointed a vengeful, mocking finger at him. The Pacers won. It was the moment of a lifetime. When he watched the tape, Miller couldn't believe his eyes. It was like being in a dream. He was flying high and knew what the defense was going to do next. He was in the zone!

TV ratings skyrocketed in Indiana, a state in which college basketball inspired more interest than the pros. Indiana University could fill the Market Square Arena faster than the Pacers. But this changed on June 1, 1994, when Miller and the Pacers became stars.

Reginald Wayne Miller came into this world on August 24, 1965, in Riverside, California. He was the second youngest of four children in a family of athletes. But he was a small child and had to wear orthopedic shoes and splints on his legs in the hopes of walking one day. The doctors weren't hopeful. Reggie spent most of his time in the kitchen with his mother. He pressed his nose against the window, enviously watching his brothers and sisters play one-on-one in the yard. His mother reassured him that he could play outside as soon as his legs got strong. He was four years old when he was freed from his metal braces and could join his siblings. His father Saul, a sergeant in the Air Force and an old high school

REGGIE MILLER
Born on August 24, 1965 in Riverside, California/6'7" 190 lbs/High School: Riverside Polytechnic/College: UCLA/Drafted by the Indiana Pacers in 1987 in the first round (eleventh overall pick)/Leader in free throws in 1991/Three All-Star Game appearances/Member of Dream Teams II and III

basketball star, took him by the hand to show him the basics of the game. Reggie learned quickly, but not fast enough to beat Cheryl, Darrell, and Tammy, who had each started to make names for themselves in their respective sports. Tammy, a volleyball player at California State, Fullerton, was a U.S. Olympic hopeful. Darrell was an excellent baseball player (he would eventually become a catcher for the California Angels), and Cheryl was becoming the Magic Johnson of women's basketball. Reggie was overshadowed. It wasn't easy for him, especially with all the talk of the others' triumphs. But he managed as best he could, and dreamed of greatness.

Every day when Reggie came home from Riverside Polytechnic High, he would practice over three hundred shots in the yard. His goal was to distinguish himself from his sister. One day, after scoring thirty-nine points in a game at school, he came home triumphantly to announce the good news. "Your sister just scored 109," his mother answered. Reggie was furious. But secretly, he worshipped Cheryl. She was Larry Bird, Michael Jordan, and Magic Johnson, he boasted, "There's never been a female player like her."

In 1984, Cheryl Miller led the U.S. women's team to the Olympic title in Los Angeles—another challenge for Reggie to live up to. At the time, he was at UCLA where whenever he missed two or three shots in a row, the crowd chanted "Cheryl, Cheryl" and his opponents stung him with, "It would be better if you asked your sister to play." He would never forget it.

Nevertheless, Reggie developed a following in college. In four years, he was the second highest scorer in UCLA history, right behind Kareem Abdul-Jabbar. As a junior, he was fourth in points scored in the NCAA, averaging 25.9 per game. During his senior year, he averaged 22.3 points for a total of 2,095 in his college career. Reggie Miller was a near perfect shooter. His only problem was confidence. When practicing alone, he forced himself to make 70 percent of his shots. It was all about rhythm and concentration. He watched the ball, never the basket, and followed its trajectory so that he could improve his next shot.

Miller was lucky enough to meet Magic Johnson while at UCLA. At that point, he wasn't sure what his future had in store; most found him a bit skinny to face the NBA giants. But Magic gave him confidence. One afternoon, he came to the school to organize a pick-up game with Byron Scott and Michael Cooper. Reggie Miller was brilliant. Afterwards, the Lakers star congratulated him and never forgot him. Magic offered Reggie advice from time to time and even introduced him to Marita Stavrou, his future wife. "He took me under his wing," explained Reggie.

It's not surprising that the Lakers had their eyes on Miller when he graduated in 1987. Unfortunately, they had the last pick, and Miller was chosen by the Indiana Pacers in the eleventh overall pick. The Indiana locals were disappointed. They had been hoping to see Steve Alford, their own star, join the team. It would take Miller seven years to become the hero we know him to be and to exorcise Cheryl's ghost. In his first year, he sank sixty-one three-point shots, beating Larry Bird's rookie record. What's more, he was the only Pacer to play in all eighty-two games of the regular season, averaging ten points per game.

Miller was consistent in upcoming seasons. In eight years, he tallied more than 20 points on average during the regular season, and more than 24 in the all-important playoffs. "Like any great player, Reggie raises the level of his game for important matches," said Pacers manager Donnie Walsh. His post-season performance puts him among the greats. On May 7, 1995, the date of the first game of the semifinals against New York, he secured his place in history. Pat Riley's team was leading by six with 16.4 seconds left in the game. Most people were leaving the Garden, thinking the game was over. But Reggie Miller was once again touched by God. In 8.9 seconds, he racked up eight points, thanks to two technical fouls and two free throws, which gave the Pacers the win. Spike Lee cursed him. Miller talked back. It was becoming a familiar scene.

Reggie is a trash-talker. He gets to people. He spends his games insulting his opponents (and their mothers) and making them lose their cool. It seems to give him motivation. He loves to be the enemy, the one people want to beat, and he even plays better when visiting other teams. In early 1991, when the Bulls were still working for their first title, Miller hurled at Jordan, "Maybe Chicago would be better off without you." Jordan exploded. But off the court, Reggie forgets it all. He knows it's only a game. He spends hours every summer counseling kids on the playgrounds, visiting children's hospitals, and

AN UNCOMMON SHOOTER (p. 225)
*Miller is an impeccable shooter. He watches the ball, never the basket,
so as to follow its trajectory and perfect his next shot.*
SPIKE PLAYS HIS PART (p. 233)
*Like many players, Spike Lee (here wearing Stark's uniform) is a trash-talker,
who taunts the Knicks' opponents. In 1994 and 1995, he spent his time bothering
Reggie Miller during the legendary meetings between New York and Indiana.*

working with charities. The kids are in awe of him.

Like many champions, Miller knows he may never win the NBA title, but he'll always have the great experience of having been on Dream Teams II and III. Also, he has given some outstanding performances while with the Pacers. He's one of the few players to have sunk more than a thousand three-pointers in his career. Only Dale Ellis has done better. He was also the first player to get more than a hundred three-pointers in six consecutive seasons (so far). He was the first Pacer to be chosen to play in an All-Star Game (in 1995). And finally, he is one of the five best free-throw shooters of all time. But all this is nothing compared to the goal he set when he was just a child practicing shots, trying to push Cheryl into the background. Reggie Miller has become a star. Not long ago, he even published an autobiography, *I Love To Be The Enemy*. A certain Knicks fan wrote the preface—Spike Lee. Supposedly, the two have become friends—that is until the next game.

IT TOOK REGGIE SEVEN YEARS TO BECOME A HERO AND TO EXORCISE THE GHOST OF HIS BIG SISTER

CHERYL

"The Mailman"

M

Karl Malone

If one day you see a huge truck on a Salt Lake City highway, check out who is in the driver's seat, because it might just be Karl Malone. He's a nature type who hates glitz. He prefers fishing, hunting, collecting old cars, and especially the wide open space in front of his thirty thousand ton truck that sports the colors of Malone Enterprises, his trucking company. Sometimes in the summer, when he has time, he'll even make deliveries himself. He loves to be on the road. The landscape, the speed, the smell of diesel—it's great. It makes him feel happy and powerful, as if no one could stop him—a little like in the NBA. Malone has been playing since 1985 and has averaged about 26 points and 11 rebounds per campaign. His "engine" has never failed and his performances are unique. But Karl Malone remembers when recruiters didn't think he was good enough. Life hasn't been easy.

Karl was born on July 24, 1963, in Summerfield, a small town in the backwoods of Louisiana. His youth was poverty-stricken. The eighth child in a family of nine, he was only four-years-old when his father took off, leaving his mother to work things out on her own. Shirley Malone worked in a saw-mill by day, and as a butcher by night while her family slept. Karl remembers seeing her put cardboard in her old shoes so that she could buy the children new ones. Although she did everything she could to provide for her family, she barely had enough to send her kids to school. Hardship forged a strong character in Karl Malone. With his brothers and sisters, he took apart an old bike, hanging one of the wheels to a tree trunk. This was their basket and the hard ground was the gym floor. Sometimes, when Karl took the bus with his mother, they would pass one of those gigantic trucks he dreamed of owning. One day, he turned to his mother and said, "When I grow up, I'll buy one like

KARL MALONE/THE MAILMAN
Born on July 24, 1963 in Summerfield, Louisiana/6'9" 255 lbs/High School: Summerfield High School/University: Louisiana Tech/Drafted by the Utah Jazz in 1985 in the first round (thirteenth overall pick)/League MVP in 1997/All-NBA First Team in 1989, 1990, 1991, 1992, 1993, 1994, 1995, 1996 and 1997/Ten All-Star Game appearances and; MVP in 1989 and 1993/Member of Dream Teams I and III

240

that." His mother smiled. "You can do it." Karl would never forget it.

Karl Malone is relentless. To this day, he continues to want his life to be an example, and this is why, despite his limited education, he was accepted into Louisiana Tech in 1981. The Bulldogs coach thought he was good, but Malone needed to work hard to become "academically eligible." After a year of intense study, he succeeded—and not just in the classroom. Karl immediately showed his power. He devoutly went to the college gym and developed amazing mobility so as to race right through his opponents. This remains his strong point.

A local journalist nicknamed him "The Mailman" for his ability "to deliver" points, assists, and rebounds. Malone finished his first season with an average of 20.9 points and 10.1 rebounds, his second with 18.8 points and 8.8 rebounds, and his third with 16.5 points and 9.3 rebounds.

In 1983, Malone was elected Louisiana Player of the Year, but NBA scouts noticed that his averages had fallen from one season to the next. Bobby Knight thought he was a good player as well, but didn't think he was good enough to represent the U.S. in the Los Angeles Olympics. Malone was cut in the trials in Bloomington, well before Stockton. This would be his last failure.

In Salt Lake City, Jazz boss Frank Layden had been watching Malone for a while, but he was only entitled to the thirteenth pick in the 1985 draft. Ultimately, this didn't matter, because no one wanted Karl Malone. Layden chose him. He knew Malone and John Stockton would be the foundation for the Utah team for the next fifteen years. It was difficult in the beginning, however. Malone felt cut off from his roots in this 92 percent white city, and spent his days on the phone. His mother encouraged him. On the court he scored 14.9 points and 8.9 rebounds on average per game for 30 minutes of game time, but failed miserably with free throws. He averaged a disastrous 48.1 percent. But Malone maintained his pride. "Do you want to be an average player, or do you want to be a star?" he repeated to himself, just as he had in college. He worked hard so that his free throw average rarely dropped below 70 percent. Nevertheless, he still asks himself if he has worked hard enough, if he has paid the price to deserve everything he now has. He says he's not so sure.

Layden pushed him. In 1986, the Jazz traded a team star, Adrian Dantley, in order to give Karl Malone a chance to bloom. The change worked. In ten years, Malone only missed four games, averaging a stellar 26 points and 10.8 rebounds per meeting. As proof of his consistency, Malone was named eight times in a row to the All-NBA First Team composed of the league's top five players of the year. He is also one of the top fifteen scorers in the history of the NBA, and was the ninth to surpass a career 20,000 points. Only four of these nine scorers have accomplished such a feat in less games than him: Chamberlain, Jordan, Robertson, and Abdul-Jabbar. Finally, Malone was voted All-Star MVP in 1989 and 1993, sharing the honor with his buddy Stockton the second time around. Chuck Daly, the Dream Team coach in Barcelona, said Malone was perhaps the strongest player in the league, both literally and figuratively speaking. "If you don't want to cut your life short, you better step aside when Karl comes out," chuckled Ricky Green, ex-guard for the Jazz. Malone had once dreamed of

TWO ARTISTS ATTACHED AT THE HIP (below)
The name Malone goes with Stockton, and vice versa.
MALONE-TYSON. THE SOUL OF A BOXER (p. 247)
Karl Malone has always been fascinated by contact sports.
He one day hopes to become Mr. Universe.
For Malone, basketball is a battle between men.

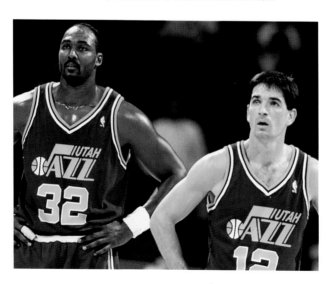

becoming Mr. Universe one day, and does in fact have some Arnold Schwarzenegger in him. "On the court, it's a man's fight," he warned, "the others can stay home with their mothers."

His ultimate goal is still the unreachable NBA title. In 1995 and 1996, he failed in the Conference Finals; in 1997, the Jazz weren't eliminated until the final game against Jordan's Bulls. But Malone was granted the title of the best player in the League in 1997—beating out Jordan. It was a brilliant achievement. Some fans have claimed that it was a conspiracy and called him an usurper. Malone replied on the court by totaling 37 points in the third game of the finals. And what about the title? When he came home to his kids, Kadee Lyn, Kylee Ann, and Karl Jr., he told himself that there were more important things in life. Malone is an anti-star, just like Stockton.

Karl Malone shares this simple life with his wife Kay, an ex-Miss Idaho. But Malone remembers his roots and he knows where his path will lead him: on the road, between Utah and his mother's Arkansas, where he has bought himself a cattle ranch. In 1992, upon his return from Barcelona, he got his commercial trucking license, plopped himself in front of the wheel of his customized eighteen wheeler, and treated himself to a twenty-six-hour trip. Not long afterwards, he also delivered a couple of tons of Idaho potatoes for Malone Enterprises. His CB handle: The Mailman. Malone likes to say that basketball is his job, and the road his life. The Mailman certainly hasn't stopped delivering.

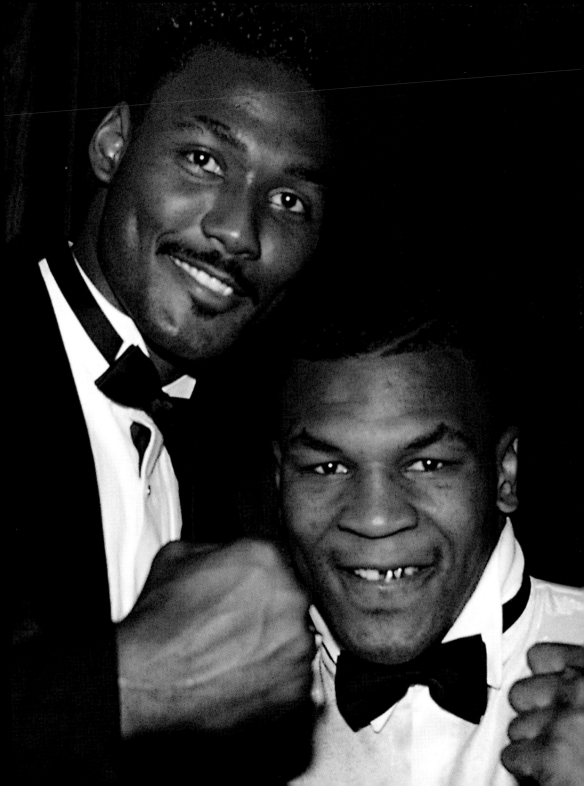

"The Reign Man"

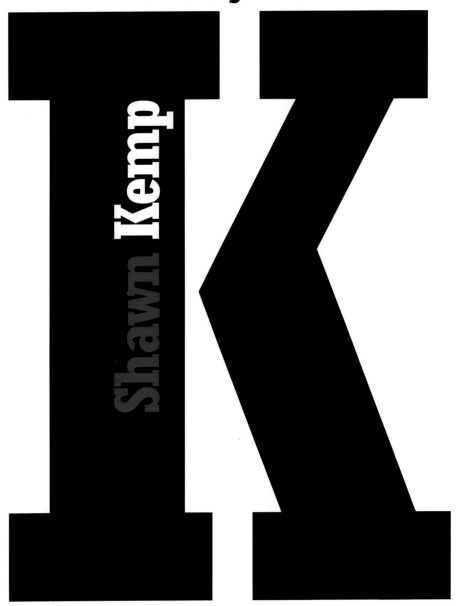

Shawn Kemp

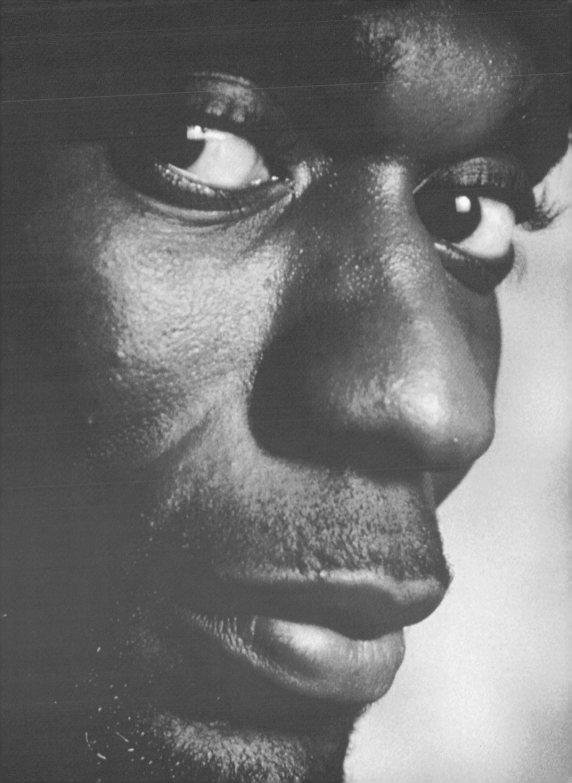

Shawn Kemp is a special player in the NBA. His ex-teammate, Michael Cage, says that if Michael Jordan weren't around, Kemp would be the kids' role model. Not long ago, however, Shawn Kemp was no more than a poster in the rooms of teenagers, a muscle-bound player good for occasionally ripping down the basketball rim in Seattle's Key arena. A lot of people couldn't understand how he had made it into the pros and become leader of the SuperSonics. Today, Kemp is one of the league's bosses, and one of the most unpredictable and spectacular players of the nineties. Magic Johnson called him the prototype for the year 2000.

Shawn Kemp was born on November 26, 1969, in Elkhart, a small industrial city on the Indiana-Michigan border. He had a happy childhood there. However, only one thing in life interested him—basketball—and this would cost him. For the young Kemp, the only good thing about school was that it had a basketball team, and that he could become a star. (This was pretty easy considering that the boy grew four inches between the ages of fourteen and fifteen. He was 6'10" at seventeen.) Concord High School swept up everything in its path. In Kemp's first year they finished first in their division, then won the Regional Final for the first time in the school's history his second year. In his senior year, the team made it into Indiana's Championship Finals.

The team scored 85 victories and 19 losses in four years. Kemp's power had no bounds. Legend has it that he once made sparks fly off the rim. Jim Hahn, the coach at Concord, was certain that Shawn was good enough to enter the NBA without going first to college, but because so few players had dared to do so, he dismissed the idea. He shouldn't have, because even if Shawn was on the cover of every local newspaper, his poor academic performance endangered his future.

SHAWN KEMP/THE REIGN MAN
Born on November 26, 1969 in Elkhart, Indiana/6'10" 256 lbs/High School: Concord High School, Elkhart/College: Trinity Junior College, Texas/Drafted in 1989 by the Seattle SuperSonics in the first round (seventeenth overall pick)/Five All-Star Game appearances/Member of Dream Team II

EVEN THOUGH THE BULLS TOOK THE 1996 NBA TITLE, WITH SHAWN KEMP, THE SONICS HAVE FOUND A LEADER

Everything went wrong for Kemp from the moment he entered college.

All the major basketball college coaches were interested in him, but Shawn chose to go to Kentucky to join the Wildcats. However, it had been a while since he'd cracked open a book, and it showed on his transcript. A law entitled Proposition 48 had recently established academic guidelines for college athletes, and Kemp found himself below the mark. He dropped out, commenting that people go to college to become doctors or lawyers and that he just wanted to play basketball. Kemp soon enrolled at Trinity Valley Community College, a less prestigious school in Texas which accepted him. Soon after he entered Trinity, he was arrested for selling stolen jewelry. Although Kemp maintained he didn't know the jewelry was stolen, he was expelled and missed a second basketball season.

In 1989, Kemp declared himself eligible for the NBA draft, but hadn't anything to show for the last two years. One of his last appearances had been at an invitation-only tournament in Las Vegas where he had placed higher than all the other young stars of his generation, not least of all Alonzo Mourning and Christian Laettner. Seattle's management was watching. When they saw this 6'10" kid weighing 220 pounds snatch rebounds, charge the basket, and shoot three-pointers, they became interested. To everyone's surprise, the SuperSonics drafted Kemp in the seventeenth overall pick.

Kemp remembers when experts claimed he would need five or six years to get used to the big leagues. It was true that he was only nineteen-years-old and only the fifth player in history to make the big jump from high school to the NBA. (Joe Grabowski, Moses Malone, Bill Willoughby, and Darryl Dawkins preceded him—not an easy list to follow.) When he arrived, he played back-up to Xavier McDaniel and watched from the bench. When he was finally brought out to play, he pulled out every stop in the hopes of seducing the coach and fans. His attempts were futile. He didn't get to play much and finished the season with an average of 6.5 points and 4.3 rebounds for his thirteen minutes of game time. Kemp's first professional year became a learning period.

Kemp began to refine his game, and in the 1990–91 season, his stats jumped to 15 points and 8.4 rebounds for thirty minutes of game time. Kemp was asserting himself. The old great, Connie Hawkins, said, "He's the modern-day forward.

Coaches of my era would never let a power forward do such things. We asked only that he grab rebounds, give the ball to the guard, and go position himself in the lane. He rips the ball away, runs across the court, and dunks, without worrying about the others. He does everything!" Kemp's progress was staggering, and the fans in the city of rain give him the nickname "The Reign Man."

Shawn Kemp's point and rebound average improved every year. In 1991, he was runner-up in the Slam-Dunk Championship and was voted to play in the 1993

A WEIGHT ON THE SHOULDERS (p. 251)
*Seattle takes a stand against Chicago and Rodman in the fourth game
of the 1996 finals. The next day, this picture is on the front page
of every newspaper in the country.*
LIFT-OFF (below)
*Kemp is one of the most wondrous players in the NBA. Michael Cage
says that if Jordan weren't around,
Kemp would be the role model.*

All-Star Game. The fans loved him. Michael Cage says that college might have helped him polish his game a bit more quickly, but it would have also taken away his spontaneity. Furthermore, no other player (aside from Jordan) had such great hang time. In 1994, the NBA selected Kemp for Dream Team II to play in the World Championships in Canada. He was appreciated for the first time.

Kemp is a shining player, but many attribute Seattle's lack of titles to his immaturity and, even more, to his lack of charisma. In the regular season, the Sonics did well but were eliminated in the first round of the playoffs. In 1994, Seattle considered trading Kemp for Scottie Pippen to try to break the pattern. The post-season losing streak lasted until 1996. After losing the first three games to Chicago in the finals, Kemp got angry. "We're cowards," he said. "We're not going to lose and get our butts kicked too!" He was not kidding around and the team got the message. The next day, Seattle punished the best team of all time. Although the Bulls won the championship, the Sonics won respect. What's better, they found a leader.

Shawn Kemp grew up in those finals, but the following year was a stormy one. Believing himself to be underpaid, Kemp at first refused to become part of the team at the start of the season, and then missed a plane when the team was playing in Sacramento. Penalties and fines piled up and Kemp's stats took a nosedive. Kemp is supposed to be a special kind of player—Jordan proclaimed him "the heart of the team," a thought that deserves consideration.

DREAM TEAM '92

"The best team of all time"

" **B**efore we see a team like this again, you won't be here anymore, and neither will I." Magic Johnson was moved. Only a few minutes earlier, he had received the gold medal in the Barcelona Olympic Games, perhaps the greatest honor of his career, and certainly the most thrilling.

The adventure began in April 1989 when the International Basketball Federation voted, 56 to 13, to send professionals to the Games. The Amateur Athletic Union of the United States, which has little or no power, complained a bit, but without consequence.

Two years later, on September 13, 1991, lightning struck when the NBA made the electrifying announcement that it would send its best players to Barcelona. People knew they would see the NBA stars on the second-rate Spanish courts, but no one expected to see such an incredible team.

On September 21st, the members of the team were announced on NBC: Magic Johnson and John Stockton would be the playmakers; Larry Bird, Michael Jordan, Chris Mullin, and Scottie Pippen would be guards and play back;

Charles Barkley and Karl Malone would play power forward; and, finally, Patrick Ewing and David Robinson would be the centers. Clyde Drexler and Duke University champion Christian Laettner would be added to the list later. The coach would be Chuck Daly.

The much hyped team was a big money-maker—but they were much more than that. First, they had a lot to make up for. As Jordan said, American basketball needed to have its dignity and pride restored. It was time to revive the glory of the 1956 Olympics in Melbourne. During those Games, a team of American college players built around Bill Russell became Olympic Champions, winning each game by an average of 53 points. It had been a sacred moment.

But since 1987, the U.S. team had done horrendously. The U.S. lost to Brazil in the finals of the Pan-American Games in Indianapolis, because Robinson and Manning couldn't stop Oscar Schmidt from scoring 46 points. In the same year, the American representatives, led by Larry Johnson and Stacey Augmon, were defeated in the World Championships by some young Yugoslavian players named Kukoc and Divac. Come time for the Seoul Olympic Games, the team was unable to recover from their last loss in Munich. They were defeated once again by the Soviet Union, 82–76, in the semifinals. And yet, these were the NBA's future stars: Robinson, Manning, Charles Smith, Mitch Richmond, Dan Majerle, Willie Anderson, Hersey Hawkins, and J. R. Reid. The misery didn't end. In 1989, the U.S. lost to Puerto Rico in the Pan-American Games, and then to the Soviet Union and Yugoslavia in the 1990 Goodwill Games. That same year, the U.S. finished only third in the World Championships. Even though Christian Laettner still believed a college team could win in Barcelona, they were haunted by a humiliating past that was too much to bear for the country that brought basketball into existence. Something had to be done, so The Dream Team was formed.

After a short 20 minute practice match against a team of college players, the Dream Team had its first official game on June 28, 1992 in Portland. Because America lost in Seoul, they had to participate in the pre-Olympic tournament for the Americas. What a joke it was.

On the day of this first game, Magic Johnson got up at 5:30 a.m., too anxious to sleep. By 10:30, he was warming up in Portland's Memorial Coliseum. He was practically alone since the game didn't start until noon. The opening ceremony had been the night before, and although it was extremely exciting, everyone was waiting for one thing: to see the best players in the world play together. From that moment on, history would be divided—before 1992 and after. The game was laughable. The U.S. beat Cuba by 79 points for a 136–57 victory! "You can't hide the sun with your finger," said Miguel Calderon Gomez, the Cuban coach. He spoke humbly but truthfully. "I don't know if there was anything really

A DREAM OF A TEAM (pp. 262–263)
The Dream Team coach surrounded by all the members. From left to right, from the top: Jordan, Bird, Magic Johnson, Mullin, Drexler, Stockton, Pippen, Laettner, Ewing, Robinson, Malone, Barkley. "Before we see a team like this again, we'll be dead and gone," says Magic.
THE PERFECT TEAM MEMBER (below)
During the Olympic games, Jordan isn't looking to be the star. He simply blends in with the rest of the team. His game-time and statistics go down.

perfect in this world, but this team sure comes close," he added. A message had been sent.

Needless to say, the Dream Team made people dream. It was built around the three best players of all time: Michael Jordan, Magic Johnson, and Larry Bird, legends who had earned a combined total of ten NBA titles. (At the time, Jordan had just won his second consecutive championship with the Bulls.) Although the International Basketball Federation and the NBA don't have the same rules, the Dream Team wasn't phased. Chuck Daly knew he had enough three-point shooters, a must when zone defense is allowed. Unfortunately, John Thompson, the coach of the American team that went to Seoul, learned this lesson the hard way.

The U.S. press didn't bother covering the other teams since, for them, the tournament *was* the Dream Team. But the matches were getting a little boring: team

DREAM TEAM III

They became Olympic champions in Atlanta, beating Yugoslavia 95–69.
Barkley says the team should be named Team USA. There's only one Dream Team,
the one that went to Barcelona.
From left to right, from the top: Robinson, Olajuwon, Pippen, Hill, O'Neal,
Payton, Malone, Miller, Stockton, Hardaway, Barkley.

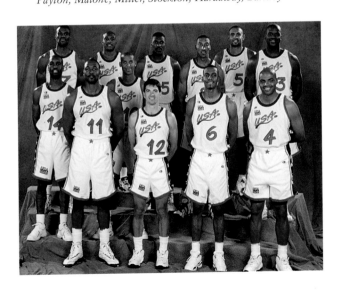

U.S.A. won 105–61 against Canada, 112–52 against Panama, 128–87 against Argentina, 119–81 against Puerto Rico in the semifinals, and 127–80 against Venezuela in the finals. Dino Radja, a Croatian and a member of the Boston Celtics, said it was best to simply take the games with a grain of salt. For most, the Dream Team could have been awarded the gold medal without bothering to compete. Germany's Hans Gnad felt that one could only hope to be lucky enough to play against them. Aware that they were ambassadors, the Dream Team was open-minded, not arrogant. They never humiliated their opponents. But even so, after their victory over Cuba, Scottie Pippen pointed out that they couldn't be expected to apologize for winning.

Each game started the same way, with the opposing team wanting a souvenir photo. Arturas Karnishovas asked his assistant coach to take a picture of him defending Barkley during the U.S.–Lithuania game. The team's feat lay not in its winning the gold, but in seducing the whole world in just two months. It was a basketball *team* that left an indelible mark on the history of the Games—not an individual athlete, swimmer, or gymnast.

During the opening ceremony, all eyes were on one person—Magic Johnson. His smile outshone everyone else's. Many asked to have their picture taken with him, and he cherished these moments. His own Olympic memories included the triumphs of Olga Korbut and Mark Spitz. Modestly, he said it was a childhood dream to stand among champions. Barcelona was charged with excitement. Many, however, lay low, like Jordan, who found a way to play golf in the mornings. But others, like Barkley, roamed the streets of Barcelona until four in the morning.

Naturally, the Americans were also the center of attention *on* the court, winning their games by an average of 43.8 points. What's more amazing is that Chuck Daly didn't call a single time-out in fourteen games (fifteen, if you include the one against France in Monaco). He explained that after a long NBA season, the players were perhaps more tired mentally than physically. The performance was there, but the heart, the enjoyable unpredictability of the game, was not. Charles Barkley said sarcastically, "Do you think we like winning all the games by 60 or 70 points? We'd rather only win by 15 points."

This wouldn't be the case even once. After an uninteresting game against Angola, ending in a 116–48 victory, the Dream Team defeated Croatia by 33 points (103–70). Yes, this was the Croatia with three NBA stars, Petrovic, Kukoc, and Radja in its ranks. This was also the team that was thought to have a chance. But it was not to be. Pippen took the opportunity to humiliate Kukoc, who had just signed with Chicago for more than what he earned himself. Kukoc finished with pathetic stats: 4 points, 2 for 11 from the field, and 7 turnovers.

After Croatia, the team defeated Germany, 111–68, producing 17 dunks. Brazil and Spain were next; they lost 127–83 and 122–81, respectively. American journalist Doug Cress lamented that the saddest thing about the games was that the Europeans had never played better. Eight or ten of their players could possibly have made it in the NBA. In the quarterfinals, Puerto Rico went down 115–77, and in the semifinals it was Lithuania with Sabonis, Khomitchous, and Kurtinaïtis who were left stranded, losing 127–76. The finals were the only thing left. The Dream Team was to play Croatia, as they had done in the preliminaries. This time the Croats were more of a challenge. In fact, they led 25–23 after ten minutes. It was an impressive ten minutes, but a half-hour later, the Dream Team won the Olympic gold, 117–85. A 32 point spread! It was a shame that the Dream Team never had the chance to face a united Yugoslavia, that would include not only Kukoc, Radja, and Petrovic but also Divac, Danilovic, Djordjevic, and Paspalj, among others. The Croatian coach, Peter Skansi, called them the Dream Team of Europe. The still-unified Soviets might also have been more of a challenge—but probably no more than that. There will never be such an extraordinary team again. Michael Jordan had foretold that the Games would remember them for a long time. But if there's only one thing that stays with us from that unforgettable summer, it has to be Magic Johnson's radiant smile as he stepped up to receive his gold medal. "Never will I forget it," he says, "never will I forget the feelings that swept through me during the national anthem. It was one of the best moments in my life."

THE DREAM TEAM'S SEASONED WARRIOR
Magic Johnson, star of the Games

CHICAGO'96

"The year records were set"

I n June 1996, during the Chicago-Seattle finals, there was one question on everyone's mind. Are the Bulls the best pro team in history? Everybody had something to say. Ex-coach Jack Ramsay, now an ESPN commentator, said Philadelphia's 1967 team was better. Others argued that the 1972 Lakers could never be matched. Jerry Sloan picked Chicago. Magic and Bird even debated the question, but didn't come to any conclusions. It was a tricky one. Although it's impossible to compare two teams from two different eras, the teams' records say something. The Bulls in 1995–1996, with seventy-two wins and ten losses, beat all the records. They even surpassed the Lakers' legendary sixty-nine and thirteen record from the 1971–1972 season. Scottie Pippen, only half-kidding, declared that the best team he played during the year was Chicago's reserve team. Michael Jordan isn't sure if he was a member of the single best team in history,

TIME OUT

Phil Jackson, surrounded by the Bulls. An ex-hippie, he protested the war in Vietnam and sometimes gives his players the Lao-Tzu to read. Jordan says he's never seen team so united in going after one goal, one destiny.

but he's certain the Bulls were one of the most amazing teams of all time.

Five days before training camp, the Bulls got some big news: Dennis Rodman, the league leader in rebounds, and the league's most flamboyant player, would be joining them. Dennis Rodman would take the Windy City by storm. Rodman said he was coming to play basketball and that was all, warning that he wasn't going to answer all the team's problems. "Besides," he said, "a basketball team is more like a computer, and you all know who the main part of the computer is." This was exactly what everyone was worried about. How would such a complicated machine function properly? Would Pippen be able to let go of the grudge he'd been holding against Rodman ever since their blow-up in 1991? Would Kukoc become sixth man without a fight? Could Longley be one of the Bulls' first strong centers? And would Jordan continue to rise to the top of the NBA, as in the past?

It didn't take long to find out the answers. In their first game against Charlotte, Jordan stacked up 42 points, Rodman grabbed 11 rebounds, and Chicago won 105–91. The next day, against Boston, Pippen was the leader in points and Kukoc in assists. The magic had begun.

All along, Phil Jackson brought the best out of his reserve players, the NBA's working class. Steve Kerr, who didn't enjoy sitting on the Bulls' bench, respected Jackson for his talent and for giving everybody a chance. It was rare. Buechler agreed, adding that his never knowing when he would play added a lot of pressure to his job. Furthermore, Jordan was more patient than before with the players on the bench. "Baseball helped me a lot. I realized that everyone can't be on the same level. I've become more understanding."

In 1996 the Bulls lost for the first time on November 14 in Orlando. This was just a little bump in the road. The next day, they gave Cleveland a beating, winning 113–94. Journalists all swear they've never seen Jordan play two bad games in a row. By mid-February, the Bulls had won forty-two games and lost only five. Jordan insisted he had no interest in the Lakers' record and that all he wanted was the title. But the press wouldn't let go of the record. Bullmania hit the U.S. In one city after another, the country went mad, buying tickets at exorbitant prices. The phenomena was compared to the excitement generated by the Rolling Stones and the Beatles. Michael Jordan had regained his invincibility. With more than 30 points on average, he was once again the league leader—and there weren't any more fights with Pippen. The two had become buddies. "The Bulls are my team," said Jordan. Pippen confirmed that they were getting along better. Before, they had a hard time letting go of their pride, but Pippen knew he had gained Jordan's respect. He was also glad not to have to bear the whole responsibility of the team anymore. He didn't quite fit the part. By April, the wins were piling up, and the loss against Charlotte on April 8 would be the last of the series. On April 14, the team beat Cleveland, winning 98–72, and tied the Lakers' record. On April 16, Milwaukee lost 86–80 and the Bulls reached the legendary 70 wins mark. There was a new slogan in Chicago: "Don't mean a thing without a ring," authored by Pippen and Harper. Soon, the slogan appeared on T-shirts.

For a while, Rodman had the best-selling book in the country, *Bad as I Wanna Be*, in which he revealed the details of his nights with Madonna. His fans adored him. After every game, he'd throw his jersey into the crowd. He said that the sport had become nothing but entertainment.

People come to watch some guys run round and round a court, just to give themselves something to do, he sneered. But Rodman behaved himself on the court, and even took home his fifth title as leader in rebounds with 14.9 per game.

Armed with Jordan, the best player and the league's leader in points scored (30.4 points per game), and Rodman, the leader in rebounds, Chicago had nothing to worry about for the playoffs. They also had Pippen, the best all-around player, Kukoc, the leading sixth man, and the best coach, Phil Jackson. What's more, Chicago had the most effective scoring offense in the league (105.2 points on average) and was the team with the largest point spread (+12.2 points on average). These stats could discourage any opponent.

In the first round of the playoffs, Pat Riley, now with Miami, played his old New York tricks, trying to provoke Rodman. It didn't work. Chicago swept 3–0, but Riley had served as a good sparring partner, as it was the Knicks who were up for the next round. Mason and Oakley were the next ones to try in vain to intimidate the Bulls. The Bulls won four games to one, Jordan running away with 44 points in the first game and 46 in the third. But he didn't carry the team alone. In the fourth and most important game, Harper, with 18 points, and Rodman, with 19 rebounds, were the ones to lead the Bulls. In the Conference Finals, the Bulls made mince-meat out of the Magic, sweeping them 4–0. Pippen said he wasn't going to apologize for winning, especially since Orlando had been the team that eliminated the Bulls the year before. In

the final game, Jordan erupted for 45 points. The only hurdle left was Seattle. The first games went as usual. Chicago won the first meeting 107–90, thanks to two unbelievable minutes in the fourth quarter from Kukoc in which he scored 10 points. He stretched the Bulls' lead from two to ten points. It had been a close call. Kukoc, who had two three-pointers, still was only 3 for 36 for the play-offs. Phil Jackson blew up, asking him whether he was planning on going for 3 for 100 or perhaps 3 for 1,000. A product of the sixties, Jackson got his strength and wisdom from Taoism. He always kept his cool and looked at the positive side of all situations. Sometimes he even gave Lao-Tzu to his players to read.

Rodman was the hero of the second game, which Chicago won 92–88. "The Worm" scored 20 points and tucked away 21 rebounds, 11 of which were offensive rebounds. This tied the record with Elvin Hayes for a finals game. He also mocked Seattle coach George Karl, who had taken a poke at him in the press only two days earlier. "Hey, are we still friends, George?" he called out in the middle of the game. It looked as if Chicago would sweep the series, especially after the third game, which was a blowout. The Bulls were leading 62–38 at the half, and wound up with a 108–86 win. Jackson was impressed with his team's

RODMANIA (p. 277)
During the 1995–96 season, Rodman made a ritual out of throwing his jersey into the crowd after each game.

strength on the road. It was a mark of their talent. Seattle's George Karl decided to loosen his rein, and encouraged his team to play as if they were on a playground. His strategy worked. Seattle won the next two games 107–86 and 89–78, forcing the Bulls to play a sixth game at the United Center. It would be the last one—a symbolic game. It was Father's Day, and Jordan, whose mind was elsewhere, left the game to his teammates. Five players accumulated more than 10 points, Rodman had 19 rebounds (11 of which were offensive again), Pippen

scored 17 points, grabbed 8 rebounds and 5 assists, and Harper, although injured, found a way to play for thirty-eight minutes, allowing the rest of the team to catch their breath.

The Bulls won it 87–75 and took their place in history. Perhaps holding that position isn't really important in the end. At the beginning of the season, Jordan said, "I'm just a guy." He's right. After all, as Charles Leroux wrote the next day in the *Chicago Tribune*, "A Stradivarius is just a violin, *Citizen Kane* is just a movie, Mount Everest is just a pile of rocks, and the Bulls are just a basketball team."

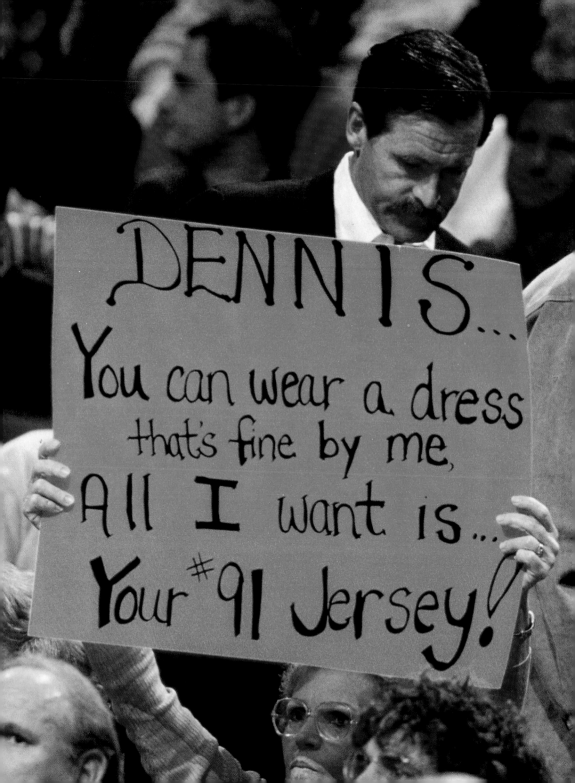

APPENDIX

NBA finals

1947	Philadelphia	beat Chicago	4–1
1948	Baltimore	beat Philadelphia	4–2
1949	Minneapolis	beat Washington	4–2
1950	Minneapolis	beat Syracuse	4–2
1951	Rochester	beat New York	4–3
1952	Minneapolis	beat New York	4–3
1953	Minneapolis	beat New York	4–1
1954	Minneapolis	beat Syracuse	4–3
1955	Syracuse	beat Fort Wayne	4–3
1956	Philadelphia	beat Fort Wayne	4–1
1957	Boston	beat St. Louis	4–3
1958	St.Louis	beat Boston	4–2
1959	Boston	beat Minneapolis	4–0
1960	Boston	beat St. Louis	4–3
1961	Boston	beat St. Louis	4–1
1962	Boston	beat Los Angeles	4–3
1963	Boston	beat Los Angeles	4–2
1964	Boston	beat San Francisco	4–1
1965	Boston	beat Los Angeles	4–1
1966	Boston	beat Los Angeles	4–3
1967	Philadelphia	beat San Francisco	4–2
1968	Boston	beat Los Angeles	4–2
1969	Boston	beat Los Angeles	4–3
1970	New York	beat Los Angeles	4–3
1971	Milwaukee	beat Baltimore	4–0
1972	Los Angeles	beat New York	4–1
1973	New York	beat Los Angeles	4–1
1974	Boston	beat Milwaukee	4–3
1975	Golden States	beat Washington	4–0
1976	Boston	beat Phoenix	4–2
1977	Portland	beat Philadelphia	4–2
1978	Washington	beat Seattle	4–3
1979	Seattle	beat Washington	4–1
1980	Los Angeles	beat Philadelphia	4–2
1981	Boston	beat Houston	4–2
1982	Los Angeles	beat Philadelphia	4–2
1983	Philadelphia	beat Los Angeles	4–0
1984	Boston	beat Los Angeles	4–3
1985	Los Angeles	beat Boston	4–2
1986	Boston	beat Houston	4–2
1987	Los Angeles	beat Boston	4–2
1988	Los Angeles	beat Detroit	4–3
1989	Detroit	beat Los Angeles	4–0
1990	Detroit	beat Portland	4–1
1991	Chicago	beat Los Angeles	4–1
1992	Chicago	beat Portland	4–2
1993	Chicago	beat Phoenix	4–2
1994	Houston	beat New York	4–3
1995	Houston	beat Orlando	4–0
1996	Chicago	beat Seattle	4–2
1997	Chicago	beat Utah	4–2

NBA Finals MVP

1969	Jerry West	Los Angeles
1970	Willis Reed	New York
1971	Kareem Abdul-Jabbar	Milwaukee
1972	Wilt Chamberlain	Los Angeles
1973	Willis Reed	New York
1974	John Havlicek	Boston
1975	Rick Barry	Golden State
1976	Jojo White	Boston
1977	Bill Walton	Portland
1978	Wes Unseld	Washington
1979	Dennis Johnson	Seattle
1980	Magic Johnson	Los Angeles
1981	Cedric Maxwell	Boston
1982	Magic Johnson	Los Angeles
1983	Moses Malone	Philadelphia
1984	Larry Bird	Boston
1985	K. Abdul-Jabbar	Los Angeles
1986	Larry Bird	Boston
1987	Magic Johnson	Los Angeles
1988	James Worthy	Los Angeles

1989	Joe Dumars	Detroit
1990	Isiah Thomas	Detroit
1991	Michael Jordan	Chicago
1992	Michael Jordan	Chicago
1993	Michael Jordan	Chicago
1994	Hakeem Olajuwon	Houston
1995	Hakeem Olajuwon	Houston
1996	Michael Jordan	Chicago
1997	Michael Jordan	Chicago

Regular season MVP

1955–56	Bob Pettit	St. Louis
1956–57	Bob Cousy	Boston
1957–58	Bill Russell	Boston
1958–59	Bob Pettit	St. Louis
1959–60	Wilt Chamberlain	Philadelphia
1960–61	Bill Russell	Boston
1961–62	Bill Russell	Boston
1962–63	Bill Russell	Boston
1963–64	Oscar Robertson	Cincinnati
1964–65	Bill Russell	Boston
1965–66	Wilt Chamberlain	Philadelphia
1966–67	Wilt Chamberlain	Philadelphia
1967–68	Wilt Chamberlain	Philadelphia
1968–69	Wes Unseld	Baltimore
1969–70	Willis Reed	New York
1970–71	Kareem Abdul-Jabbar	Milwaukee
1971–72	Kareem Abdul-Jabbar	Milwaukee
1972–73	Dave Cowens	Boston
1973–74	Kareem Abdul-Jabbar	Milwaukee
1974–75	Bob McAdoo	Buffalo
1975–76	Kareem Abdul-Jabbar	L.A.
1976–77	Kareem Abdul-Jabbar	L.A.
1977–78	Bill Walton	Portland
1978–79	Moses Malone	Houston
1979–80	Kareem Abdul-Jabbar	L.A.
1980–81	Julius Erving	Philadelphia
1981–82	Moses Malone	Houston
1982–83	Moses Malone	Philadelphia
1983–84	Larry Bird	Boston
1984–85	Larry Bird	Boston
1985–86	Larry Bird	Boston
1986–97	Magic Johnson	Los Angeles
1987–88	Michael Jordan	Chicago
1988–89	Magic Johnson	Los Angeles

1989–90	Magic Johnson	Los Angeles
1990–91	Michael Jordan	Chicago
1991–92	Michael Jordan	Chicago
1992–93	Charles Barkley	Phoenix
1993–94	Hakeem Olajuwon	Houston
1994–95	David Robinson	San Antonio
1995–96	Michael Jordan	Chicago
1996–97	Karl Malone	Utah

Coach of the year

1962–63	Harry Gallatin	St. Louis
1963–64	Alex Hannum	San Francisco
1964–65	Red Auerbach	Boston
1965–66	Dolph Schayes	Philadelphia
1966–67	Johnny Kerr	Chicago
1967–68	Richie Guerin	St. Louis
1968–69	Gene Shue	Baltimore
1969–70	Red Holzman	New York
1970–71	Dick Motta	Chicago
1971–72	Bill Sharman	Los Angeles
1972–73	Tom Heinsohn	Boston
1973–74	Ray Scott	Detroit
1974–75	Phil Johnson	K.C./Omaha
1975–76	Bill Fitch	Cleveland
1976–77	Tom Nissalke	Houston
1977–78	Hubie Brown	Atlanta
1978–79	Cotton Fitzsimmons	Kansas City
1979–80	Bill Fitch	Boston
1980–81	Jack McKinney	Indiana
1981–82	Gene Shue	Washington
1982–83	Don Nelson	Milwaukee
1983–84	Frank Layden	Utah
1984–85	Don Nelson	Milwaukee
1985–86	Mike Fratello	Atlanta
1986–97	Mike Schuler	Portland
1987–88	Doug Moe	Denver
1988–89	Cotton Fitzsimmons	Phoenix
1989–90	Pat Riley	Los Angeles
1990–91	Don Chaney	Houston
1991–92	Don Nelson	Golden State
1992–93	Pat Riley	New York
1993–94	Lenny Wilkens	Atlanta
1994–95	Del Harris	Los Angeles
1995–96	Phil Jackson	Chicago
1996–97	Pat Riley	Miami

Rookie of the year

1952–53	Don Meineke	Fort Wayne
1953–54	Ray Felix	Baltimore
1954–55	Bob Pettit	Milwaukee
1955–56	Maurice Stokes	Rochester
1956–57	Tom Heinsohn	Boston
1957–58	Woody Sauldsberry	Philadelphia
1958–59	Elgin Baylor	Minneapolis
1959–60	Wilt Chamberlain	Philadelphia
1960–61	Oscar Robertson	Cincinnati
1961–62	Walt Bellamy	Chicago
1962–63	Terry Dischinger	Chicago
1963–64	Jerry Lucas	Cincinnati
1964–65	Willis Reed	New York
1965–66	Rick Barry	San Francisco
1966–67	Dave Bing	Detroit
1967–68	Earl Monroe	Baltimore
1968–69	Wes Unseld	Baltimore
1969–70	Kareem Abdul-Jabbar	Milwaukee
1970–71	Dave Cowens	Boston
	Geoff Petrie	Portland
1971–72	Sidney Wicks	Portland
1972–73	Bob McAdoo	Buffalo
1973–74	Ernie DiGregorio	Buffalo
1974–75	Keith Wilkes	Golden States
1975–76	Alvan Adams	Phoenix
1976–77	Adrian Dantley	Buffalo
1977–78	Walter Davis	Phoenix
1978–79	Phil Ford	Kansas City
1979–80	Larry Bird	Boston
1980–81	Darrell Griffith	Utah
1981–82	Buck Williams	New Jersey
1982–83	Terry Cummings	San Diego
1983–84	Ralph Sampson	Houston
1984–85	Michael Jordan	Chicago
1985–86	Patrick Ewing	New York
1986–97	Chuck Person	Indiana
1987–88	Mark Jackson	New York
1988–89	Mitch Richmond	Golden State
1989–90	David Robinson	San Antonio
1990–91	Derrick Coleman	New Jersey
1991–92	Larry Johnson	Charlotte
1992–93	Shaquille O'Neal	Orlando
1993–94	Chris Webber	Golden State
1994–95	Grant Hill	Detroit
	Jason Kidd	Dallas
1995–96	Damon Stoudamire	Toronto
1996–97	Allen Iverson	Philadelphia

Defensive Player of the year

1982–83	Sidney Moncrief	Milwaukee
1983–84	Sidney Moncrief	Milwaukee
1984–85	Mark Eaton	Utah
1985–86	Alvin Roberston	San Antonio
1986–97	Michael Cooper	Los Angeles
1987–88	Michael Jordan	Chicago
1988–89	Mark Eaton	Utah
1989–90	Dennis Rodman	Detroit
1990–91	Dennis Rodman	Detroit
1991–92	David Robinson	San Antonio
1992–93	Hakeem Olajuwon	Houston
1993–94	Hakeem Olajuwon	Houston
1994–95	Dikembe Mutombo	Denver
1995–96	Gary Payton	Seattle
1996–97	Dikembe Mutombo	Atlanta

Leader in Points Scored

1946–47	1389	Joe Fulks	Philadelphia
1947–48	1007	Max Zaslofsky	Chicago
1948–49	1698	George Mikan	Minneapolis
1949–50	1865	George Mikan	Minneapolis
1950–51	1932	George Mikan	Minneapolis
1951–52	1674	Paul Arizin	Philadelphia
1952–53	1564	Neil Johnston	Philadelphia
1953–54	1759	Neil Johnston	Philadelphia
1954–55	1631	Neil Johnston	Philadelphia
1955–56	1849	Bob Pettit	St. Louis
1956–57	1817	Paul Arizin	Philadelphia
1957–58	2001	George Yardley	Detroit
1958–59	2105	Bob Pettit	St. Louis
1959–60	2707	Wilt Chamberlain	Philadelphia
1960–61	3033	Wilt Chamberlain	Philadelphia
1961–62	4029	Wilt Chamberlain	Philadelphia
1962–63	3586	Wilt Chamberlain	San Francisco
1963–64	2948	Wilt Chamberlain	San Francisco
1964–65	2534	Wilt Chamberlain	S.F.-Philadelphia
1965–66	2649	Wilt Chamberlain	Philadelphia
1966–67	2775	Rick Barry	San Francisco
1967–68	2142	Dave Bing	Detroit
1968–69	2327	Elving Hayes	San Diego

1969–70*	31.2	Jerry West	Los Angeles
1970–71	31.7	Kareem Abdul-Jabbar	Milwaukee
1971–72	34.8	Kareem Abdul-Jabbar	Milwaukee
1972–73	34.0	Nate Archibald	K.C./Omaha
1973–74	30.6	Bob McAdoo	Buffalo
1974–75	34.5	Bob McAdoo	Buffalo
1975–76	31.1	Bob McAdoo	Buffalo
1976–77	31.1	Pete Maravich	New Orleans
1977–78	27.2	George Gervin	San Antonio
1978–79	29.6	George Gervin	San Antonio
1979–80	33.1	George Gervin	San Antonio
1980–81	30.7	Adrian Dantley	Utah
1981–82	32.3	George Gervin	San Antonio
1982–83	28.4	Alex English	Denver
1983–84	30.6	Adrian Dantley	Utah
1984–85	32.9	Bernard King	New York
1985–86	30.3	Dominique Wilkins	Atlanta
1986–87	37.1	Michael Jordan	Chicago
1987–88	35.0	Michael Jordan	Chicago
1988–89	32.5	Michael Jordan	Chicago
1989–90	33.6	Michael Jordan	Chicago
1990–91	31.5	Michael Jordan	Chicago
1991–92	30.1	Michael Jordan	Chicago
1992–93	32.6	Michael Jordan	Chicago
1993–94	29.8	David Robinson	San Antonio
1994–95	29.3	Shaquille O'Neal	Orlando
1995–96	30.4	Michael Jordan	Chicago
1996–97	29.6	Michael Jordan	Chicago

Leader in Rebounds

1950–51	1080	Dolph Schayes	Syracuse
1951–52	880	Larry Foust	Fort Wayne
		Mel Hutchins	Milwaukee
1952–53	1007	George Mikan	Minneapolis
1953–54	1098	Harry Gallatin	New York
1954–55	1085	Neil Johnston	Philadelphia
1955–56	1164	Bob Pettit	St.Louis
1956–57	1256	Maurice Stockes	Rochester
1957–58	1564	Bill Russell	Boston
1958–59	1612	Bill Russell	Boston
1959–60	1941	Wilt Chamberlain	Philadelphia
1960–61	2149	Wilt Chamberlain	Philadelphia
1961–62	2052	Wilt Chamberlain	Philadelphia
1962–63	1946	Wilt Chamberlain	San Francisco
1963–64	1930	Bill Russell	Boston
1964–65	1878	Bill Russell	Boston
1965–66	1943	Wilt Chamberlain	Philadelphia
1966–67	1957	Wilt Chamberlain	Philadelphia
1967–68	1952	Wilt Chamberlain	Philadelphia
1968–69	1712	Wilt Chamberlain	Los Angeles
1969–70*	16.9	Elving Hayes	San Diego
1970–71	18.2	Wilt Chamberlain	Los Angeles
1971–72	19.2	Wilt Chamberlain	Los Angeles
1972–73	18.6	Wilt Chamberlain	Los Angeles
1973–74	18.1	Elving Hayes	Capital
1974–75	14.8	Wes Unseld	Washington
1975–76	16.9	Kareem Abdul-Jabbar	Los Angeles
1976–77	14.4	Bill Walton	Portland
1977–78	15.7	Len Robinson	New Orleans
1978–79	17.6	Moses Malone	Houston
1979–80	15.0	Swen Nater	San Diego
1980–81	14.8	Moses Malone	Houston
1981–82	14.7	Moses Malone	Houston
1982–83	15.3	Moses Malone	Philadelphia
1983–84	13.4	Moses Malone	Philadelphia
1984–85	13.1	Moses Malone	Philadelphia
1985–86	13.1	Bill Laimbeer	Detroit
1986–87	14.6	Charles Barkley	Philadelphia
1987–88	13.03	Michael Cage	Los Angeles
1988–89	13.5	Hakeem Olajuwon	Houston
1989–90	14.0	Hakeem Olajuwon	Houston
1990–91	13.0	David Robinson	San Antonio
1991–92	18.7	Dennis Rodman	Detroit
1992–93	18.3	Dennis Rodman	Detroit
1993–94	17.3	Dennis Rodman	San Antonio
1994–95	16.8	Dennis Rodman	San Antonio
1995–96	14.9	Dennis Rodman	San Antonio
1996–97	16.1	Dennis Rodman	Chicago

Leader in Assists

1946–47	202	Ernie Calvery	Providence
1947–48	120	Howie Dallmar	Philadelphia
1948–49	321	Bob Davies	Rochester
1949–50	396	Dick McGuire	New York
1950–51	414	Andy Phillip	Philadelphia
1951–52	539	Andy Phillip	Philadelphia
1952–53	547	Bob Cousy	Boston
1953–54	518	Bob Cousy	Boston
1954–55	557	Bob Cousy	Boston
1955–56	642	Bob Cousy	Boston

1956–57	478	Bob Cousy	Boston
1957–58	463	Bob Cousy	Boston
1958–59	557	Bob Cousy	Boston
1959–60	715	Bob Cousy	Boston
1960–61	690	Oscar Robertson	Cincinnati
1961–62	899	Oscar Robertson	Cincinnati
1962–63	825	Guy Rodgers	San Francisco
1963–64	868	Oscar Robertson	Cincinnati
1964–65	861	Oscar Robertson	Cincinnati
1965–66	847	Oscar Robertson	Cincinnati
1966–67	908	Guy Rodgers	Chicago
1967–68	702	Wilt Chamberlain	Philadelphia
1968–69	772	Oscar Robertson	Cincinnati
1969–70*	9.1	Lenny Wilkens	Seattle
1970–71	10.1	Norm Van Lier	Cincinnati
1971–72	9.7	Jerry West	Los Angeles
1972–73	11.4	Nate Archibald	K.C./Omaha
1973–74	8.2	Ernie DiGregorio	Buffalo
1974–75	8.0	Kevin Porter	Washington
1975–76	8.1	Don Watts	Seattle
1976–77	8.5	Don Buse	Indiana
1977–78	10.2	Kevin Porter	Detroit-New Jersey
1978–79	13.4	Kevin Porter	Detroit
1979–80	10.1	Michael Ray Richardson	New York
1980–81	9.1	Kevin Porter	Washington
1981–82	9.6	Johnny Moore	San Antonio
1982–83	10.5	Magic Johnson	Los Angeles
1983–84	13.1	Magic Johnson	Los Angeles
1984–85	14.0	Isiah Thomas	Detroit
1985–86	12.6	Magic Johnson	Los Angeles
1986–87	12.2	Magic Johnson	Los Angeles
1987–88	13.8	John Stockon	Utah
1988–89	13.6	John Stockon	Utah
1989–90	14.5	John Stockon	Utah

1990–91	14.2	John Stockon	Utah
1991–92	13.7	John Stockon	Utah
1992–93	12.0	John Stockon	Utah
1993–94	12.6	John Stockon	Utah
1994–95	12.3	John Stockon	Utah
1995–96	11.2	John Stockon	Utah
1996–97	11.5	Mark Jackson	Indiana

Leader in Blocked Shots

1973–74	4.85	Elmore Smith	Los Angeles
1974–75	3.26	Kareem Abdul-Jabbar	Milwaukee
1975–76	4.12	Kareem Abdul-Jabbar	Los Angeles
1976–77	3.25	Bill Walton	Portland
1977–78	3.38	George Johnson	New Jersey
1978–79	3.95	Kareem Abdul-Jabbar	Los Angeles
1979–80	3.41	Kareem Abdul-Jabbar	Los Angeles
1980–81	3.39	George Johnson	San Antonio
1981–82	3.12	George Johnson	San Antonio
1982–83	4.29	Tree Rollins	Atlanta
1983–84	4.28	Mark Eaton	Utah
1984–85	5.56	Mark Eaton	Utah
1985–86	4.96	Manute Bol	Washington
1986–87	4.06	Mark Eaton	Utah
1987–88	3.71	Mark Eaton	Utah
1988–89	4.31	Manute Bol	Golden State
1989–90	4.59	Hakeem Olajuwon	Houston
1990–91	3.95	Hakeem Olajuwon	Houston
1991–92	4.49	David Robinson	San Antonio
1992–93	4.17	Hakeem Olajuwon	Houston
1993–94	4.10	Dikembe Mutombo	Denver
1994–95	3.91	Dikembe Mutombo	Denver
1995–96	4.49	Dikembe Mutombo	Denver
1996–97	3.44	Shawn Bradley	Dallas

Best Game Performances

POINTS

Wilt Chamberlain	Philadelphia	against New York	at Hershey PA.	March 8, 1962	100
Wilt Chamberlain	Philadelphia	against Los Angeles	at Philadelphia	December 8, 1961	78
Wilt Chamberlain	Philadelphia	against Chicago	at Philadelphia	January 13, 1962	73
Wilt Chamberlain	San Francisco		at New York	November 16, 1962	73
David Thompson	Denver		at Detroit	April 9, 1978	73
Wilt Chamberlain	San Francisco		at Los Angeles	November 3, 1962	72
Elgin Baylor	Los Angeles		at New York	November 15, 1960	71
David Robinson	San Antonio		at L.A. Clippers	April 24, 1994	71

| Wilt Chamberlain | San Francisco | | at Syracuse | March 10, 1963 | 70 |
| Michael Jordan | Chicago | | at Cleveland | March 28, 1990 | 69 |

REBOUNDS

Wilt Chamberlain	Philadelphia	against Boston	at Philadelphia	November 24, 1960	55
Bill Russell	Boston	against Syracuse	at Boston	February 5, 1960	51
Bill Russell	Boston	against Philadelphia	at Boston	November 16, 1957	49
Bill Russell	Boston	against Detroit	at Providence	March 11, 1965	49
Wilt Chamberlain	Philadelphia	against Syracuse	at Philadelphia	February 6, 1960	45
Wilt Chamberlain	Philadelphia	against Los Angeles	at Philadelphia	January 21, 1961	45
Wilt Chamberlain	Philadelphia	against New York	at Philadelphia	November 10, 1959	43
Wilt Chamberlain	Philadelphia	against Los Angeles	at Philadelphia	December 8, 1961	43
Bill Russell	Boston	against Los Angeles	at Boston	January 20, 1963	43
Wilt Chamberlain	Philadelphia	against Boston	at Philadelphia	March 6, 1965	43

ASSISTS

Scott Skiles	Orlando	against Denver	at Orlando	December 30, 1990	30
Kevin Porter	New Jersey	against Houston	at New Jersey	February 24, 1978	29
Bob Cousy	Boston	against Minneapolis	at Boston	February 27, 1959	28
Guy Rodgers	San Francisco	against St. Louis	at San Francisco	March 14, 1963	28
John Stockton	Utah	against San Antonio		January 15, 1991	28
Geoff Huston	Cleveland	against Golden State	at Cleveland	January 27, 1982	27
John Stockton	Utah		at New York	December 19, 1989	27
John Stockton	Utah	against Portland		April 14, 1988	26
Ernie DiGregorio	Buffalo		at Portland	January 1, 1974	25
Kevin Porter	Detroit	against Boston	at Detroit	March 9, 1979	25
Kevin Porter	Detroit		at Phoenix	April 1, 1979	25
Isiah Thomas	Detroit	against Dallas		February 13, 1985	25
Nate McMillan	Seattle	against L.A. Clippers		February 23, 1987	25
Kevin Johnson	Phoenix	against San Antonio		April 6, 1994	25

Olympic Medals

	GOLD	SILVER	BRONZE.
1936	USA	Canada	Mexico
1948	USA	France	Brazil
1952	USA	USSR	Uruguay
1956	USA	USSR	Uruguay
1960	USA	USSR	Brazil
1964	USA	USSR	Brazil
1968	USA	Yugoslavia	USSR
1972	USSR	USA	Cuba
1976	USA	Yugoslavia	USSR
1980	Yugoslavia	Italy	USSR
1984	USA	Spain	Yugoslavia
1988	USSR	Yugoslavia	USA
1992	USA	Croatia	Lithuania
1996	USA	Croatia	Lithuania

World Championships

		1	2	3
Buenos Aires	1950	Argentina	USA	Chile
Rio de Janeiro	1954	USA	Brazil	Philippines
Santiago	1959	Brazil	USA	Chile
Rio de Janeiro	1963	Brazil	Yugoslavia	USSR
Montevideo	1967	USSR	Yugoslavia	Brazil
Ljubljana	1970	Yugoslavia	Brazil	USSR
Puerto Rico	1974	USSR	Yugoslavia	USA
Manila	1978	Yugoslavia	USSR	Brazil
Cali	1982	USSR	USA	Yugoslavia
Madrid	1986	USA	USSR	Yugoslavia
Buenos Aires	1990	Yugoslavia	USSR	USA
Toronto	1994	USA	Russia	Croatia

Eric Besnard is the International reporter for Canal+ television, France. He has covered NBA games in the U.S. since 1990 and has met some of the best basketball players of all time.

This book could not have been written without the invaluable help of Sebastien Ratto Viviani. Many thanks.
Thanks also to:
Thierry Marchand, journalist for *L'Équipe*
Eric Weinstein, NBA
George Eddy, reporter at Canal+
Grégoire Margotton, reporter at Canal+
Stéphane Mislin, reporter at Canal+
Didier Le Corre, journalist for *Basket News*
Arnaud Lecomte, journalist for *L'Équipe*
Jean-Jacques Vervialle, Canal+ stats
Dominique Bessières, Canal+ stats
Ray Lalonde, NBA Europe
Veronique Marchal, NBA U.S.A

Video Archives:
Canal+
Credits © NBA photos